Up Sims Creek

The First 100 Trips

D1431480

By Rodney Nelson
Almont, North Dakota Rancher

Illustrated by Scott Nelson
Solen, North Dakota Rancher

For additional information on books and tapes by Rod Nelson,
or to book him as your next banquet speaker, contact him at:
> Rod Nelson
> 4905 44th St.
> Almont, ND 58520
> (701) 843-8081

This book is dedicated to my wife
Teri, better known as "The Missus."

Table of Contents

Up Sims Creek

By: Rod Nelson

"Survival 101" for Ranchers: Finding Off-Ranch Income

Times are tough here at Sims. The natives claim it's been downhill ever since they took us off the map in 1947 and changed our address to Almont.

I had to renew my loan the other day. My loan officer told me to bring my 1994 income tax returns when I came in. Usually a somewhat dour fellow, he brightened up considerably when he saw the $50 profit I made ranching last year. After dancing on his desk for a few minutes he grabbed my hand and congratulated me, his voice choking with emotion. I wiped his eyes, patted him on the back and led him back to his chair so we could continue the business at hand.

Things went well. It wasn't more than four hours later he agreed to finance my operation one more year – but he did recommend I either expand my operation or find some additional off-ranch income.

I reflected on the wisdom of his advice as I drove home. I knew he was right. I didn't really care to jump right in to more cattle and had little enthusiasm for overthrowing any of my neighbors at that time. Besides, I still hadn't trained all of the cows I have now to eat leafy spurge.

Plan B was the answer, so I loaded old Ben, picked up my friend Ross for company and headed for Gillette, WY to a big team roping. It rained all the way and the old Dodge really ran rough. I'm not real mechanical, but I think it either had emphysema or TB. We bucked a fierce headwind from Belle Fourche to Gillette which really slowed us down.

Ross loved every bit of it. He has an active interest in antelope. He punched me in the ribs and pointed to each antelope he saw. South Dakota was tolerable. But, 40 miles into Wyoming, I had a dent in my side the size of a Toyota garage. I finally made Ross get out and walk. He was a good sport about it and stopped and waited now and then so he never got out of sight.

"Survival 101" for Ranchers: Finding Off-Ranch Income

It was still raining when we got there and there were only outside stalls left for my horse. When I came back to feed him I thought it was strange he laid down so soon – then I saw he hadn't. Wyoming gumbo gets soft in the rain.

Two pots of coffee and an enormous supper later we hit the sack. I slept poorly. Was it the coffee, the anticipation, or the rock crusher sounds Ross made all night?

Old Ben fared better. He looked OK, though he sounded quite a bit like my Dodge.

Ross was quite an asset when I saddled up. He shoveled a trench under Ben so I could get the cinches through.

I found some better ground for warming Ben up, but by the time the roping started he had more mud on him than a Red River Valley four-wheel drive.

Now I won't say I roped poorly, but by the time I missed for my second partner, several of my fans broke down and wept openly in the stands.

The bright spot in my weekend was my Dodge. It ran like a well-oiled watch all the way home. Figuring entry fees, gas, motel and eats, expenses came to about $460. However, if I'd stayed home, I calculated I'd have wrecked $550 worth of machinery, and I had at least $200 worth of entertainment and experience. So there it is, a tidy $290 weekend profit, not even counting the pickup improvements.

I rode out and checked my cows the next morning. Despite the fact there is more grass out there than I have seen in 11 years, I noticed they still looked like they had wintered in Somalia. A quote I heard from a fella in Gillette came to mind. A wise man once said, "If you don't change directions you will wind up where you are headed." As I pulled up on a hill to give my horse a breather and gazed out over my operation, the wisdom of these words struck me . . . . If I'm gonna survive, I've got to enter more ropings.

Up Sims Creek

By: Rod Nelson

Putting the Lid on Overhead Requires Generous Neighbors

Times are tough here at Sims. I can't even afford a threshing machine to decorate my highest hill. The best I can do is drag a dead cow up there now and then. They don't last as long, but they look just as good.

In an effort to keep a lid on costs, I decided a few years ago that rather than pay interest on high priced machinery, I would just borrow the stuff. This is an excellent method, but it does have some drawbacks.

First of all – you need very generous neighbors. Second – they must have better equipment than you, and last, and perhaps most important, they must be mechanical enough to repair any equipment you break so it is in top shape the next time you need to borrow it.

Beware of the neighbor who doesn't come over and retrieve his machinery now and then from your yard. This machinery wears out quickly.

This brings to mind the silage wagon I borrowed from my good neighbor Johnson. If he would have only driven over and retrieved his wagon and done a few minor repairs, he would still have his wagon. Instead, he relied on me to fix and return it.

It was swept away in the July flash flood of '93. Actually, I believe it was defective, as any good wagon should be able to float a half mile and crash into a RR bridge without damage.

The bottom line is the change in my long range plan – I no longer raise corn. The good news is I no longer have to borrow my neighbor Jacobson's corn planter and cultivator.

Another thing I have noticed is some of the people I have borrowed from extensively have taken to farming at night when they buy a new piece of machinery. This and

3

Putting the Lid on Overhead Requires Generous Neighbors

the guard dogs they use to patrol their machinery lots have done much to prevent me from surging right into 21st century ag technology.

Some of my friends, in an effort to get a lid on their own expenses, have decided it is better to give me their old equipment rather than loan me the new stuff.

I was desperate for a new drill this spring, as the 10-foot Case Drill Johnson gave me in '85 was completely shot. I called my friend Erickson (always a dependable source of machinery).

"Hey Pard," I said. "Do you have any drills I could get from you?"

"Nope," he said, then, "wait a minute, I think I have one out in the shelter belt."

"What color is it?" I asked.

"Green," he said, "with yellow lids."

I paused, my heart racing with excitement. I had never dreamed of having anything that modern. After my speech returned, I told him I'd be up to get it the next day.

I was at my loan officer's desk early the next morning. After giving him the titles to two pickups and one car he agreed to loan me the gas money for a round trip to Minot.

Erickson was ready when I arrived and led me through a heavy stand of pigweed and brush to the drill. "Shucks," I said, "don't you have a grass seeder for it? I need to seed some alfalfa."

"Just run the seed on top of the ground and harrow it in," he replied, "You do have a harrow, don't you?"

"Yeah," I said, "don't you remember, you gave me one two years ago."

Putting the Lid on Overhead Requires Generous Neighbors

We soon had the drill loaded on a borrowed trailer. Erickson whistled as he walked around it. "Wow! I didn't remember it was in such good shape! All the discs turn and everything!"

I countered by pointing out one tire that was completely shot. I was gunning the engine on my Dodge when he was mumbling something about how he'd like me to give back the drill transport. His mouth was still flapping when I sprayed gravel over him and hit the road. It's best to leave before they get too nostalgic.

What an investment! Normally that 80 acres I farm is the toughest month of the year for me, but this year, with 14-foot equipment, I finished seeding May 31st. A Sims record.

A good farmer once told me it takes good equipment to be a good farmer. How true that is, and think how good that drill will look on my depreciation schedule!

Up Sims Creek

By: Rod Nelson

No Emotion or Brand Loyalty – Just Prejudice

Times are tough here at Sims. I'm so far behind in my work I haven't even had any hay rained on yet.

It's a funny thing, although I can understand preferences people have for certain breeds like maybe Percherons, Thoroughbreds, or Norwegians. I am just not mechanical enough to understand the loyalty some people have toward makes of automobiles or brands of machinery.

After all, how excited can you get about something that doesn't nicker a greeting or dig up the flower bed.

The only real emotion I have for certain makes or models is the prejudice I feel against them.

Take that Dodge pickup of mine, for instance. I believe the suspension on that machine was designed by a group of chiropractors just to drum up business. I've been thrown from quite a few saddle broncs that were smoother riding than that Dodge.

It doesn't run that grand either.

A fella that was riding with me a couple weeks ago said, "This must be a water truck – it runs good downhill." It really does run good downhill so in the hilly country I am well satisfied with it 50 percent of the time. I guess that is why it still is my favorite vehicle.

I have a '79 Ford that doesn't exactly give me goosebumps either. I'd like it alot better if it wasn't so darn injury-prone.

Everything happens to it. The hood flies open in heavy traffic, trees fall on it, every rock in the country can hardly wait to lie in front of it, horses will leave second-cut

No Emotion or Brand Loyalty – Just Prejudice

alfalfa just to eat the paint off the hood and bulls will jump three fences and fight their way through a mile of thick brush just to scratch their backs on the rear view mirror.

I have seen well-mannered children, their faces scrubbed and beaming with innocence, riding their bikes to Sunday School, suddenly making a U-turn back to that Ford just to kick out a headlight.

A great improvement on that model would have been a built-in tow bar, as I'm always pulling it somewhere for repairs. I wish I had one horse on the place that is so well broke to lead.

Chevrolets have never intrigued me much. My Grandpa bought a new 1940 Chevrolet car. It turned out to be a lemon and we've pretty much held it against them ever since.

In the interest of fairness, however, I did buy a 1967 Chevrolet pickup in 1983. I thought they deserved a second chance. I drove that thing for 10 years and sure enough – the blasted outfit wore out. They won't get another chance from me.

My brother had an International pickup once. That was a pretty tough outfit. It seemed to hold together remarkably well, however it had some weak points.

It would sink right down to the axles in a half inch of fresh snow and I'd say you could fire a schoolteacher easier than start that pickup on a cloudy day.

International used to have a TV ad that showed a proud International owner driving his pickup across incredibly rough ground at tremendous speed.

When Brother saw that ad he would always comment, "I know just how that guy feels, he has probably spent all morning trying to start that thing and he's not going to slow up for nothin'."

No Emotion or Brand Loyalty – Just Prejudice

Someone is always telling me that if I bought a new pickup I might be happier, but if I bought a new one I wouldn't be able to afford to drive it farther than the mailbox. Besides, I took out a 30-year loan when I bought that used Dodge so unless I come across a mighty good deal, I'll be driving it awhile.

Wish they still built Studebakers – I wouldn't mind trying one.

Up Sims Creek

By: Rod Nelson

Milk Cows – They're Profitable and Also Recreational

Times are tough here at Sims. The cost of gain is going to be high this year, the grass is so good I can't get my cows to graze the neighbor's CRP.

People often ask me, "Just where is Almont?" The easiest explanation is to say we are 15 miles southwest of the big cow west of Mandan. Everyone seems to remember the big Holstein cow.

Folks in New Salem take their Holsteins very seriously. They even use the Holstein as their school mascot. Evidently when they had to decide on a school mascot, they took note of other area mascots, like the Eagles, Wildcats, Warriors and Rattlers and decided they too would like a mascot that epitomized athleticism.

Almost all the ranchers around Towner milked a few cows when I was a kid. Looking back it is easy to visualize these creatures as "athletic." Many were great fence crawlers, a few were good high jumpers. We had some that could kick with deadly accuracy, and almost all of them could switch you right in the eye when you sat down to milk.

Strangely enough, despite all that, they seemed to have a hard time hitting the gutter.

Back at that time, there weren't many "straight Holsteins" in our area. In fact, we really preferred Hereford-cross milk cows. They seemed to buck considerably better and were a lot more comfortable to ride.

Riding a purebred Holstein is comparable to straddling a sharp axe.

My dad was a somewhat "casual" dairyman and as long as we milked the cows, he had no verbal objection to us riding the milking herd. We boys were fairly conscientious however, as we almost always milked them before we took them to the arena.

Bullropes, rosin, leather gloves and spurs hung in the barn with the rest of the

9

Milk Cows – They're Profitable and Also Recreational

milking equipment. If we had a serious discussion about milk cows, it wasn't about butterfat or pounds of milk produced. It was more likely about whether or not she bucked straight or turned back, or maybe if she was good or bad in the chute.

Dad didn't seem to have traditional views on dairying. He always said that the profit in milking came not from the cream sold, but the money you saved by being forced to stay home and milk them. Also, he said it was nice to have something the boys could complain about right away in the morning.

Most of the folks in our neighborhood were pretty casual with the milk chores. Those were good rugged cows, not like the finicky modern milk producers. And if you weren't right on time to milk, it didn't seem to matter.

Like my old friend Ricky once said, "It's a darn poor cow that can't hold two days' milk."

Our cows led a good life. They usually were around 'til they reached a ripe old age and often had the winters off – just like the range cows. Nowadays, the dairymen around New Salem cull them just for being poor milk producers!

Yes, those old cows were not only athletic, they helped produce some athletes as well. Many a firm handshake was developed milking – or riding those cows. I can never remember a cow being culled for being a "hard" milker.

Dairymen have few better friends around than me. I can't even guess how much butter and cheese I've eaten.

I can eat butter on almost everything – I just won't take a chance on eating poorly lubricated food. A neighbor lady offered me a low fat cookie a couple days ago. I said, "You wouldn't happen to have some nice creamy butter, would you?"

Up Sims Creek

By: Rod Nelson

The "Nelson Method" – It Really Works and That's No Bull

Times are tough here at Sims. The other night, I dreamt I was 37 again. That would have been fine if I hadn't still been a junior in high school.

I figure it's time for a little more educational column. This is the time of year when it's time to take your bulls, or your neighbor's bulls, out of your pasture. If you are really fussy, it may be time to take your bulls out of your neighbor's pasture.

If there is a good set of corrals nearby there is usually no problem; however, corrals are not always available. In such a case, the ambitious operator hauls a few tons of portable corrals to the area and directs the setup operation. I have never cared much for this. In the first place, I only have three panels that match. Besides, it's just too hard on the missus.

The adventurous operator loads horse and the missus, drives close to the bull, unloads horse, ropes bull and drags bull to trailer. He then has missus thread rope through side of trailer and has her twist bulls tail when he drags him in. This usually works but occasionally the bull makes a big arc on the end of the rope and caves in the side of pickup and/or trailer, wipes out the rearview mirror and at least one taillight. The missus gets flattened out a couple times as well. When this happens both the cowboy and bull suffer considerable abuse. This isn't a bad method but it is hard on horses, equipment, and man-wife relationships. It also makes the missus smell funny when she gets back in the pickup.

The semi-lazy operator has bulls so gentle you merely walk up to them, halter them and lead them in the trailer. This method definitely lacks class.

The truly lazy operator lines them out with the pickup and runs them into the neighbor's pasture and picks them up when the neighbor gathers in the fall. When he does pick them up, he always has a puzzled look on his face and claims they were all in two days ago. This method also lacks class but does show some imagination.

The "Nelson Method"– It Really Works and That's No Bull

The worst operator runs his bulls with the cows year-round. This type wonders why he doesn't have a uniform calf crop.

I like to use the "Nelson Method." Actually I learned this from a fella by the name of Joel Nelson from Alpine, TX. (It's hard to believe a North Dakotan could learn anything from a Texan, but this method really does work.)

You merely drive out to the pasture and park your trailer along a fence, preferably a stretch with a few solid posts and most wires intact. Then ride out and chase your bull gently to the back of the trailer. At this point ride away for a minute or so. When you return the bull will most often run away. Run the bull as hard as you can for 300 to 400 yards, then cut him off and ease him back at a walk to the back of the trailer where you again leave him alone for a minute or so. Keep repeating this process, each time running the bull a shorter distance. Never try to crowd the bull into the trailer. He will soon learn the trailer is "Kings X" and will be willing and eager to head for the trailer. Don't be in a hurry to dash up and shut the trailer gate when he jumps in the first time. If he does come out he will really be easy to load the next time and will stay in.

Several bulls can be loaded in the trailer at the same time.

This method really works and saves a lot of wear and tear on man and beast unless you are riding a clumsy horse and he falls down in a couple rock piles.

A bull will usually load in 20 minutes or so the first time and each time gets quicker and easier. After once or twice, you can park the trailer in the middle of the pasture and the bull will go right in it.

I have never tried this using a motorcycle or three-wheeler, but it may make good watching.

Try it – you'll like it. Good luck.

Up Sims Creek

By: Rod Nelson

Old Cowboy Helps Induct Good Cowboy into Hall of Fame

Times are tough here at Sims. I've been slam dunked three times in two weeks. it is so sad to see an old fella get bucked off, especially when you see it that close.

I had a rare honor last week. Brad Gjermundson, four-time World Champion Saddle Bronc Rider from Marshall, ND, was inducted into the Pro Rodeo Hall of Fame and he asked me to make his introductory speech.

Public speaking rarely bothers me, but I'll admit this job had me somewhat nervous. It is no small thing to be inducted into this hall. Brad is the first North Dakotan to receive this honor, and I wanted to find the appropriate words to use in this five-minute speech.

In a rare spirit of preparation, I started organizing my thoughts on the plane en route to Colorado Springs, but the thoughts didn't come easily.

His accomplishments in rodeo are impressive. He was North Dakota High School Champion, Collegiate National Champion, NDRA Champion, PRCA Rookie of the Year and four-time World Champion Bronc Rider. Along the way he has won such prestigious rodeos as Houston, Denver, San Antonio, Pendleton, Cheyenne, Frontier Days, The Calgary Stampede and the list goes on.

Brad has a quiet way about him and you won't find him seeking the limelight, but he is truly one of the great riders, not only of this time, but of all time.

Through the '80s, North Dakotans enjoyed cheering Brad on at the National Finals Rodeo, so it was disappointing that he didn't show up at the NFR for several years.

About a year ago I talked to Brad and told him I thought he could still be as good a bronc rider as he ever was, but he had to face the facts – he was no kid anymore. He was 35 years old and probably should be considering some serious commitment to physical conditioning, probably some running or weight training or something.

Old Cowboy Helps Induct Good Cowboy into Hall of Fame

Brad agreed that I was probably right and promised he would give it some thought.

After Brad's fantastic return to the NFR in 1994 and winning well over $80,000, I called to congratulate him and mentioned that the physical training might have been a factor in his success.

"Well," Brad said, "I really didn't do a whole lot."

"Didn't you run or anything?" I asked.

"Nope," he said, but then brightening up a bit, he added, "but I have been doing some sit-ups."

"Great," I said, "How many?"

"Well, not too many, just one every morning when I get out of bed."

Brad has been an inspiration to many young riders around the state and certainly an inspiration to the rest of us as well.

A couple of years ago I went to Brad and said, "You know, Brad, I've got a darn good notion to lose 25 pounds, go to one of your bronc riding schools just to freshen up a bit, and see if I could be the oldest guy in history to win the "World."

"Well, Rod," he said. "I think you have a darn good chance of losing that 25 pounds."

It was a nice ceremony. Well over 50 North Dakotans made the trek to Colorado Springs for the ceremony.

I mentioned some of the above points and hope I did justice to the occasion.

I traveled down there in a six-passenger plane. Of the five North Dakotans in that

Old Cowboy Helps Induct Good Cowboy into Hall of Fame

plane, three were pilots. I was honored when the pilot of the plane asked me to sit in the front seat with him. I assumed at the time he judged me to be competent to take over the controls in the event of an emergency and was duly disappointed to learn later he merely wanted most of the weight in the front of the plane.

It was an exciting flight. We flew into thunderstorms both ways. Never an enthusiastic flier, I was amazed at the damage I inflicted on the seat cushions of that plane. It just goes to show, you don't need teeth to bite hard when you're nervous.

I was mighty glad to see "Terra Firma." I'll take my chances riding colts anytime.

Up Sims Creek

By: Rod Nelson

Want a "White Water" Experience?: Then Come to Sims

Times are tough here at Sims. Got a letter from the U.S. Postal Service the other day informing me that my new address is Rodney Nelson, 4905 44th Street, Almont, ND. Now my address here at Sims is longer than Main Street.

Summer is fading away almost as fast as the paint on my horse trailer. It's no big deal for me, but I feel sorry for those who live for summer water sports. It is such a short season in North Dakota.

Most all the recreation I have participated in has involved clouds of choking dust, but that is not to say we don't have water sports here at Sims.

I read the other day about Princess Di, on vacation somewhere in the American West. She and her sons were there for a "White Water" experience.

They should have come to Sims. Lots of white water here. Merely run a glass of our well water and there it is – white water! You can pass a lot of time waiting for the white to settle out. For longer lasting viewing pleasure merely let the glass air dry and the white spots are there all the time.

Strangely enough this "White Water" makes the blackest coffee you have ever seen. Let it sit for a few minutes and it will create an oil slick that would make the Exxon Valdez green with envy.

I have been criticized at times for lack of ambition, but I'd say anyone who can drink two pots of that stuff each morning before stepping outside has to have plenty of fortitude.

One of the family favorites is "Shower Sports." They wait till I jump in the shower, then they dash to the kitchen sink and alternate running cold and hot water. At first a little, so they can imagine me frantically adjusting the faucet knobs, then when I

Want a "White Water" Experience?: Then Come to Sims

think I finally have it just right, they send me blasts of scalding or freezing water. They seem to love the sound of me ricocheting off the end of the shower stall. It's noisier than branding yearlings in a squeeze chute, they say.

Even the livestock seem to get into the spirit of "Water Sports." It's funny how they can sense those times when you are really late for something and barely have time for that "quick" shower. Just when you are fully lathered, cows that have been lying around all day chewing their cuds will suddenly develop a powerful, unquenchable thirst. What a feeling to see the water pressure drop to a pitiful trickle, then stop altogether.

It's nothing around here to see a fully lathered family member sprinting naked through the snowdrifts in a blizzard, clear a couple fences like an Olympic hurdler, beat off a herd of cows from the water fountain with a shower brush, slam the lids on the fountain and be back under the shower head by the time the water is running again.

I suppose it looks a little funny. I know the Schwan Man seems to get quite a kick out of it.

We got rural water here last spring. It's made quite a difference in our lives.

What a pleasure it is, not to come home late from the field and have the missus meet me at the door, her lips drawn back over her teeth like a Pit Bull, and say those terrible words, "We have no water."

What a pleasure it is for the missus not to have to hear my stories of how my Great-Grandmother never complained about hitching her ox to the stoneboat and going a mile to the creek for a barrel of water.

Now the most screaming around here is once a month when we get the water bill!

Up Sims Creek

By: Rod Nelson

End of "Windy" Season at Sims Will Be Welcomed

Times are tough here at Sims. I got that yellow Toyota and the missus back in 1980. I still have both of them and can't afford a tune up for either one.

I'm looking forward to the weather change this fall. Many people dread the fall and winter, but for me it's a time of great relief. It signals the end of the "windy" season.

The windy season usually starts here at Sims on the first really nice warm summer day. It almost always takes me by surprise. I'll be working around the yard, pleasantly sweating, when I become aware of a humming sound. This sound increases gradually in intensity until it becomes a great throbbing roar!

It's with a heavy heart I head to the house and carefully unlatch the screen door, holding tight so it isn't blown from my grasp. I pull my hat down hard over my eyes to shield them from flying objects and, bending sharply at the waist, I struggle against the wind until I reach my chair.

The missus is dashing up and down the stairs, crawling along the walls checking the outlets. Each time a vacant outlet is found another fan cord is frantically jammed in, and she is off for another.

She isn't satisfied until every fan in her collection (at least 150) is shuddering and blowing somewhere. We have fans in the ceiling, fans on the tables, tall ones that stand on the floors, window fans, door fans, you name it we have it.

The place sounds like a jet airplane testing ground.

Reading a paper is only accomplished by folding and refolding until it's the size of a book of matches. Even then it's best to clamp it to the table with a vice grip so it won't blow away.

End of "Windy" Season at Sims Will Be Welcomed

I keep a couple 18-inch pipe wrenches on the kitchen table all summer just to lay on top of my pancakes or they'll sail around the place like Frisbees.

Sleep is almost impossible. However, I've found if I use ear muffs for the noise and toss a couple log chains across the bed to hold the blankets down, I can get by.

The missus tries to arrange the fans so there is no place in the house to get out of the wind.

I wish I could plant a shelter belt across the living room. Next summer I am at least going to build some sort of windbreak with corral boards in front of my chair.

It seems like the missus has only two wishes. She wants to be cold in the summer and hot in the winter.

The missus really outdid herself one day! She put so many fans in one room, there was absolutely no place for the wind to go. The wind all ran into itself, then it just collapsed, fell on the floor and got quiet.

I notice the missus already has quite a pile of firewood split and stacked. Looks like another long, hot winter!

Up Sims Creek

By: Rod Nelson

Learning to Deal With Fine-Tuned Nerve Endings

Times are picking up here at Sims. I'm getting a nice start at haying.

One of the drawbacks of this ranching business is the day-to-day pain that we have to deal with. I'm not referring to the emotional pain, which would be the type of pain you would feel if your wife could no longer handle two five-gallon feed pails in each hand. No, I'm referring to the plain old miserable physical pain that we ranchers have to contend with most days.

It's a rare day when we aren't trampled, burned, hit with some type of flying debris, squashed, hammered or suffer some other type of injury. I have never been real fond of pain and it's not getting any better as I get older.

My brother always said that I have the pain threshold of a canary. He enjoyed ridiculing my pain intolerance and took pride in the fact that he was tougher than me. I don't think he was tough at all. He merely didn't feel pain. You could drop an anvil on his head and he never seemed to notice.

My dad, now he was tough. I remember once when nailing steel on a roof, he hit his thumb so hard he blew red meat out both sides of his thumb. Never said a word – just kept on working. When I noticed his thumb at dinner, I asked him why he hadn't said anything. He just said that it hurt so bad he didn't think it would help to mention it.

I am one of the unfortunate few who have wonderfully tuned nerve endings, truly getting the most pain out of each injury.

Feeling pain so intensely has forced me to develop ways in which to handle it. Many people react to pain with childish displays of cursing, screaming, an hopping about, which tapers off to puppy-like whimpering after ten minutes or so. I never lower myself to such levels unless there is a large crowd around.

Learning to Deal With Fine-Tuned Nerve Endings

I can handle moderate to severe pain quite stoically if I'm alone. For severe pain, however, I often resort to the tight circle method.

Most pain we suffer is self-inflicted. It's nearly always a by-product of carelessness like falling off slippery things while wearing the wrong footwear, or mentioning the fit of the missus' overalls when she has a hoe in her hand.

Most of these types of pain can be handled with the tight-circle method. Merely hobbling in increasingly smaller circles muttering to yourself, "Why?! Why?! How could I be so stupid?"

Evidently I use this method alot. When my son was about three years old, a horse stepped on my foot, ripping the big toe nail completely off. A couple days later I was tamping a post with my son. He had his "very own" tamping bar, which he used with much enthusiasm and little accuracy. When the inevitable happened, I went into a tirade usually reserved for large assemblies.

Leaning nonchalantly on his tamping bar and with a heavy sigh, he commented, "Just make a couple tight circles, Dad. You'll be OK."

For accidents that result in large loss of hide and really intense pain, I use the old "Fetal Position" method. This is a last resort and I only use it if the tight circle method fails to bring relief.

I was in the fetal position the other day, lying in some weeds behind the shop, when my daughter arrived with Kool-Aid and cookies.

"How did you find me here," I asked through clenched teeth.

"Oh, easy," she said breezily. "Mom told me to bring your lunch to the shop and if you weren't there, to just follow the blood trail."

Sometimes I wish I hadn't been blessed with such finely-tuned nerve endings!

Up Sims Creek

By: Rod Nelson

LAS (Lutefisk Addiction Syndrome) Common Among Norwegians, Germans

Times are tough here at Sims. I've reached the age when my knees buckle and my belt won't.

Excitement is at a fever pitch again in Almont. The annual Lutefisk and Lefse Supper is coming up on November 4, and the town is bracing itself for the hordes of lutefisk eaters.

The Lutefisk Supper in Almont is a community event. Most of the local people and quite a few workers from the surrounding area pitch in and devote many hours to make this event possible. Some just like to work. Others love working in an area heavily scented with lutefisk.

On an average year, this town of 100 or so will serve 800-900 people . . . election years we allow for an influx of politicians. Every North Dakota politician that ever amounted to anything has eaten here.

Lutefisk is a Norwegian tradition. Norwegians eat the stuff because they like to eat it, and because of the health benefits of eating food soaked in melted butter.

Almont is a small Norwegian community. However, they did some experimental cross-breeding with Germans in the late 1940s. They find that crossbreeds are not quite as smart as "straight" Norwegians, but they have a heavier haircoat and seem to winter better. That, however, is another story.

Norwegians account for only part of the annual lutefisk crowd. Many full-blooded Germans are regulars. They had seen what lutefisk had done for the Norwegians and desperately wanted some for themselves. Norwegians through the centuries have adapted to eating the stuff and can take it or leave it. Many Germans, sadly enough, have developed LAS (lutefisk addiction syndrome).

LAS (Lutefisk Addiction Syndrome) Common Among Norwegians, Germans

Symptoms of LAS include loose jaws, heavy salivation with excessive drooling, and a vacant, staring look in the eyes. The only cure for LAS is massive doses of lutefisk. It is a proven scientific fact that no one can eat more lutefisk than a German with LAS. With lutefisk well over $3/lb. in 1995, this creates quite a problem. If it weren't for the fact that a certain German from New Salem comes over the day before and peels a lot of potatoes, we would offer him an expense-paid trip to Disneyland just to save on lutefisk.

Some, like North Dakota Public Service Commissioner Leo Reinbold, originally came to campaign. Now he comes because he just can't help himself.

Almont has a reputation for the very finest lutefisk. Credit is certainly due to Head Lutefisk Cook Olson. A tall, imposing fella, wielding a big lutefisk probing fork, Olson is indisputably the "King of the Kitchen." Many people feel Olson should have been a veterinarian. They feel if he can do all that for lutefisk, he certainly could come up with a cure for the scours.

Olson is assisted by No. 2 Cook Johnson and No. 3 Cook, yours truly, Nelson. Johnson mainly disposes of used lutefisk water and does other common jobs. I am there because it is as far away from where they wash pots and pans as I can get. Also, I'm a backup for Johnson, an injury-prone fella, who has been involved in some nasty lutefisk accidents in past years and has had to go home.

The Lutefisk and Lefse Supper is a great event for Almont, marred only by the criminal element it brings to town – namely the lefse thieves.

Lefse thieves are usually, but not always, women. They may be any one of several types.

Type A is the brazen thief. This type feels the world owes them lefse, and will openly stuff their pockets during the meal.

LAS (Lutefisk Addiction Syndrome) Common Among Norwegians, Germans

Type B wouldn't consider stealing anything all year, but finds an irresistible urge at a lutefisk supper. This type will grab a sheet of lefse and pretend it is a napkin, perhaps spreading it on her lap for awhile, then will casually crumple it up, wipe her mouth with it, blow her nose and clean her classes with it, before tucking it into her brassiere. She will repeat this process many times during the meal. She feels no one knows; however, everyone enjoys watching Type B.

Type C uses an accomplice. Most often it is her husband who creates a diversion. He typically fakes a heart attack and thrashes around on the floor a bit. When the crowd gathers, she will dump a couple of platters of lefse in her purse. Type C is uncommon, but will raise heck with the lefse supply when they show up.

Lutefisk thieves are rare, but beware of the woman who arrives with the plastic-lined purse. These people are popular only with cats.

No one has ever apprehended a lutefisk or lefse thief. They are just too much fun to watch.

It has been said that lutefisk is made from cod fish, but I don't know if that has ever been proven. At any rate, it is truly the "Breakfast of Champions," and to Norwegians it is the "other white meat."

Up Sims Creek

By: Rod Nelson

Nelson's Old Friend, Rudy, the Cow Dog, Goes to Heaven

Times are tough here at Sims. Rudy, the cow dog, is dead. Found him at death's door the other day, and I had to help him through. It was the least I could do for my old friend.

I had him 14 years, only one year less than the missus. I've spent a lot of time through the years trying to train both of them. I was finally making a little progress with Rudy. It's not that the missus hasn't learned a lot, it's just that she doesn't like taking orders from me.

Ol' Rudy never seemed to mind taking orders. He never paid attention to any of them anyway.

Whatever his shortcomings, Rudy was no ordinary dog. Ordinary dogs will in time learn to watch a gate. Rudy did, too. In fact, he could watch a hundred cows walk single file through one and would never stop the cows unless you were trying to chase them through it. Rudy liked to chase cattle, not guard gates. He probably reasoned it was job security to let them through. He knew I would darn sure need him to get the cattle back out of the stockyard. He loved running them back out – through the gate or through the fence.

Ordinary dogs like to mark tires. Rudy enjoyed that too, but when my neighbor Joel drove his pickup in my yard, Rudy always marked the windshield! Not just the windshield, but always on the driver's side. I'll always remember the glum look on Joel's face as he scraped the yellow ice off on cold winter days.

Probably one of Rudy's greatest accomplishments was teaching us to understand dog language. To the casual observer it may have sounded like ordinary barking, but he had a special bark for every occasion.

There was a "car over the Sims hill" bark, a "car coming down the driveway" bark,

26

Nelson's Old Friend, Rudy the Cow Dog, Goes to Heaven

the "horses are eating in the window boxes" bark and the "carload of Jehovah's Witnesses are here" bark.

I probably liked him the best when he got so old he mainly hung around the porch. He wasn't able to get into much trouble. He got so he couldn't even catch a cat anymore.

Ol' Rudy caught lots of heck from me, but he never held it against me. No matter how rough I got with him, he was always glad to see me. He was always my friend.

I've entertained lots of people with the poem I wrote about Rudy. I tried it once after he died, but it wasn't the same. The only good part is that I know I can still write one more about him. You will be able to find it in my third book, which I'll call "Rudy Goes to Heaven," or something like that.

Speaking of books, my second book, "Cowboy Laundry," is hot off the press. I'm embarrassed to say the missus is charging $7.50 plus $1 for postage. Grossly overpriced I'd say – but no use arguing with the missus. She's not as understanding as Rudy.

Up Sims Creek

By: Rod Nelson

I'll Ask for Less, But It's Likely I'll Get More

Times are tough here at Sims. Sold my calves. Need I say more? Actually, I got a good price. However, it was about $100 per head less than I needed. Looks like I may have to ask for less this Christmas.

I'd ask for less this Christmas,
But it may be asking for too much –
Like less around my middle
And less aches and pains and such.

Less debt would sure be dandy,
Less work is on the list –
And in the next election
Less campaigning I'd insist.

Less wind is a priority,
For sure less snow and ice,
And next spring when I am calving
Less scours would be nice.

Less hair loss – naw, I'd settle
For less jokes about my hair,
And less time to find old pictures
To prove it once was there!

Less meanness in my cowherd,
This I'd ask for sure -
Or less panic in the missus
When they are chasing her.

Less need to beg for credit,
Less bankers to support,
Or less grumbling and complaining
When my payment comes up short.

Less mosquitoes in the Summer,
Less Winter in the Fall,
This list could go forever
Should I name them all.

It's just not realistic,
I'd have a better chance, I'd guess
If I'd ask for more of these things
Instead of asking for less.

Up Sims Creek

By: Rod Nelson

New Year's Resolutions to Live With (And Get By With)

Times are so tough here at Sims, my bank sent a sympathy card along with my last bank statement.

Wanted to buy the missus something really special for Christmas this year so I decided to ask an old friend for advice. "Why don't you buy her something you can see through?" he said.

I agreed that would be a good idea, but after checking prices I decided to buy her long underwear instead. She'll just have to wait 'til cattle prices improve before she gets that new screen door.

Sure has been a nice holiday season. Absolutely beautiful winter weather here in Morton County with just enough snow to make things bright and clean looking. Any more snow and we wouldn't be able to see all the bones the dogs have worked so hard to collect and display in the front yard.

Good winter weather helps put one in the holiday mood and makes holiday traditions even more enjoyable.

One tradition we have is that my daughter and I always buy our Christmas tree. We spent 41 seconds this year and finally chose one that cost $7.42 with tax. We were quite proud of it, but a couple of people insinuated I was a cheapskate for not spending more and getting a "fuller" tree.

I didn't explain, but I wish they could understand that I'd like a tree that looks like a "real" tree. A tree that had to "try" a little to make a living. A tree that maybe grew up on thin soil like I did.

A tree that maybe grew on the edge where the wind blew a little harder. A tree that didn't look like it had been injected with steroids or plastered with makeup. A tree that didn't look like an upside down ice cream cone.

New Year's Resolutions to Live With (And Get By With)

Besides, Annika and I had enough money left so we could buy a little lunch before we came home.

A favorite tradition of ours is spending many days eating a variety of foods, most of which are soaked with butter, cream, or both. High fat foods are tasty in the wintertime and they help keep you warm.

Regardless of what kind of a year 1995 may have been, we have to go on with 1996. I have always thought the start of the new year is a great time, if for no other reason than to imagine we are starting with a clean slate and have the opportunity to make good new year's resolutions. I've made several new year's resolutions myself.

#1. I will take the missus on just as many Caribbean cruises as I did last year.

#2. I will buy the missus just as many furs as I bought her last year.

#3. I will try to get more work out of my kids.

#4. I will hug the missus every time she patches my coveralls.

#5. I will haul another load of well-rotted manure to the missus' garden.

#6. I will lose 35 pounds.

The last resolution I will enjoy the most, as I have a wonderful stack of good Wranglers on the top shelf of the closet just waiting for me to return to the appropriate size.

I have taken the liberty of getting a head start on the weight loss and have started a diet and exercise program already, in fact, I dieted and exercised throughout the holiday season.

New Year's Resolutions to Live With (And Get By With)

It's a bit hard to find a proper exercise program when you don't have any of those modern machines to work out on. I would really like to run, but when I do run I have trouble sleeping, as my knees tend to glow in the dark.

About all I can do is walk. It's a bit of a problem as I am 46 miles from the mall. I have to be content with walking around Dolly's pasture. It's about four miles or so.

The hardest part is the one mile of the walk that is on the main road to Almont. It's easy walking, but everyone wants to give me a ride.

I try to walk real early before many people are on the road, but the mailman always sees me and it kills him to not be able to help me out. It's getting so I can wave him by, but he still slows down enough so I can see him shaking his head in disbelief.

Even total strangers hit the brakes and back up. "Having trouble?" they ask. "Naw, just out for a walk," I reply. "Are you sure?" "Yup, I'm just trying to lose a little weight," I reassure them.

"Do you want to get in and warm up?" is another common offer. "No, I'm doing fine," I say. Before they drive off they'll offer me everything from hot chocolate to Hershey bars, but no one wants to believe I am walking for exercise.

I figure my body is the only thing I have clear title to and I better try to take care of it, as it's easy to let it get out of shape.

Like my old friend Laverne Kreft once said, "I don't gain much, just a pound or so a year, but by golly after 50 years or so it tends to add up."

Happy New Year.

Up Sims Creek

By: Rod Nelson

The Hood Of '49 Kaiser Was "The Ultimate Thrill Machine"

Times are tough here at Sims. Only have one neighbor I can keep up with. He doesn't have anything either.

I spent a night in Avon, CO, last week. My room was paid for, but I happened to glance at the rate posted on the door. I was amazed to see the room rate was $545/night. The hotel was basically a ski resort with the lifts right outside the door. There were people there from Japan and England and all over the United States.

It's kind of hard to imagine people having that kind of money to spend on winter sports. Add lift tickets, equipment and perhaps helicopter rides to the very top for the real thrill seekers, and you are talking big money.

I guess North Dakotans are able to spend plenty for winter thrills as well, as you see plenty of brand new snowmobiles around the country, some costing well up into the thousands of dollars.

I doubt if I would ever spend very much for winter thrills, even if I had cash to burn. It's not because I don't like winter, it's just that I have already had thrills enough for a lifetime and it didn't cost much at all.

Back when I was a kid we had the ultimate thrill machine. It was the hood off of a 1949 Kaiser, powered by the strongest, fastest horses we had on the ranch. Once you got some speed up, you could put that horse in a tight circle and have that hood sailing out at the end of the rope somewhere near Mach One.

The only safety feature the hood had was a little hay tossed down for some padding. Everything else was pure danger. I don't remember what we had to hang on to, but we hung on for dear life to something, as it was no fun to be thrown out of the thing at top speed.

The Hood Of '49 Kaiser Was "The Ultimate Thrill Machine"

My brother was four years older than me and rarely would he ever include me in "fun" things, but he always wanted to include me when he wanted to do some "carhooding."

"Wanna go for a car hood ride?" he'd say. "Will you go slow?" I'd ask hopefully. "Absolutely," he'd say, "just a nice trot." "Promise," I'd beg. He'd stick his hands in his pockets and vow that he'd give me the nicest, safest ride ever. I'd finally climb in the hood and we'd be off.

It was grand, especially in fresh, soft snow. The hood would bob and weave along, whispering through the snow. Gosh, it felt good. It was a wonderful sensation. Then all of a sudden big brother would turn around in the saddle. "Having fun?" he'd say. "You bet, this is great!" I'd reply. Then all of a sudden his eyes would get kind of a yellow glaze, his teeth would flash in a ghoulish grin, and he'd lean over the saddle horn, lashing the horse with the reins. We went from pleasure to pure terror in a fraction of a second. Four hooves at that speed threw snowballs back at you like a Gattling Gun. He'd take me over the biggest drifts as fast as he could, then send me sliding sideways into clumps of wild rose bushes at incredible speeds. Then, when you felt you had survived the absolute worst tortures and would dare to peek up over the hood and look ahead, you'd realize the worst was yet to come. "No. No. Please, no!" I'd scream as he'd bear down on a spot on the prairie where Dad had been feeding cows. He could always find a spot where there was about a jillion frozen cow turds and loved to send me careening over them.

The tremendous racket of that hood pounding over those frozen cow pies was overshadowed only by the peals of hideous laughter coming from Brother.

He was always eager to take his turn in the hood. I generally gave him nice rides as he tended to pound me soft if I didn't.

One day though, I was loping across the meadow with him in tow and I saw a place

The Hood Of '49 Kaiser Was "The Ultimate Thrill Machine"

where Dad had dug out a hay stack. The snow had drifted up into some tremendous banks. Old Keno gave me all he had on the straight-away and I put him into a perfect turn, the hood swinging out there so fast it almost pulled Keno off his feet. It was wonderful to see the look of horror in Brother's eyes. The freckles on his ashen face looked as big as 50 cent pieces as the huge drift came to meet him. I can still see him lose his grip as the hood shot straight up in the air. Both he and the hood spun in the air a long time before they lit again on the frozen January prairie.

Life was grand that day. Paybacks are wonderful!

Up Sims Creek

By: Rod Nelson

Stranded in Motel Room Gives One Time to Pause and Reflect

Times are tough here at Sims. Millions of people this time of year find entertainment by gluing themselves to the TV for the Super Bowl. I'm happy enough this time of year if I'm not stuck on the toilet bowl!

I had quite a vacation in Fargo two weeks ago. Right after the Country Woman of the Year luncheon, I-94 was closed due to a blizzard. I was barely able to get to a motel room as the storm got fierce quickly and visibility was soon reduced to almost nothing, even in town.

It was interesting in a way. It is rare that I have ever been in a situation where I had more money than I needed. I had 20 bucks burning a hole in my pocket for two days and no place to spend it.

I have always enjoyed winter storms when I am home, but found alot less pleasure in them when stuck in a Fargo motel with nothing to do. It did give me time to sit back and think.

I thought back 25 years to when I was going to school in Fargo. I was driving an 11-year-old Rambler at that time.

Dad gave me that car. He bought it at a sheriff's sale for $50. The last owner had driven it into a tree or something else solid. The hood and one fender were smashed. I got a hood and fender off an old white car to fix my new black one. My friends at NDSU called it the "Skunk Wagon."

As I sat in my motel room I thought of how my fortunes had improved in the last 25 years. I no longer had an 11-year-old Rambler out in the parking lot. Now I had an 11-year-old Buick.

I thought back to the old Rambler and how it would start in any kind of weather. I

36

Stranded in Motel Room Gives One Time to Pause and Reflect

also thought of my Buick that I had been jumping and cranking on for two days with no success.

Once, years ago, on a 40 below day, a friend who had always ridiculed my Rambler called and asked if I could help him start his new GTO.

"Could you come over and give us a pull," he asked.

"Well, Carl, how do you know my car will start?" I asked.

"It'll start," Carl replied grudgingly.

Of course it started. It was with smug satisfaction that I pulled the new GTO down University Drive with my "Skunk Wagon" until it started.

I thought of the engine block heater that I never got around to installing on my Buick. I thought of all the methods I could have used to start the thing if I had been home. I especially thought of my space heater and my battery charger.

I thought of things I would do if I was President of the United States. The first thing I would do is make a rule that all cars had to have a standard transmission and big hook where you could hook up your team of horses. In fact, it would be illegal to sell any vehicle you couldn't start with a team.

Naturally, I thought of my missus and kids home alone at Sims. I thought of how terribly lonesome they must be for me. I also admit I felt a little smug as I felt they finally would have to admit how much they needed me. I called home bracing myself for the lonely, wistful, forlorn voices I expected to hear.

"Hi, Dad. Where are you?" my son answered.

Stranded in Motel Room Gives One Time to Pause and Reflect

"I'm in Fargo," I said.

"Oh, we thought you went to town for parts or something."

"Well, how is everything?" I asked.

"Great," he said. "Joel came over and fed the cows, everything is fine."

"Do you miss me?" I asked.

"Yeah, sure Dad. And don't forget my basketball game Saturday."

Life goes on at Sims.

Up Sims Creek

By: Rod Nelson

There's a Difference Between "Registered" and "Grade" Pups

Times are tough here at Sims, but it could be worse. I thought we had a bit of a cold snap here, but I heard of a fella from Marshall, ND, that set a pan of hot water outside on February 1 and it froze so fast the ice was still warm.

I got a new dog a week or so ago. Ever since old Rudy passed on, the missus has been dropping little hints like how she didn't want any pups around in the winter time and how she hates house-training pups. I bought one anyway.

We named him Reuben. Guess we should have called him Geyser, as he goes off so regularly.

The missus loves him anyway, but the house-training methods we use are different than we used to use.

Years ago when Rudy was a pup, the main training method was to rub the pup's nose in the piddle and throw him out the door. The missus claims that is too cruel for the '90s. Now she rubs my nose in it and throws me out. She claims if the pup sees it enough he'll catch on. I don't know if the pup is learning anything, but he sure seems to get a kick out of it.

I got me a registered pup this time. I've had plain old "grade" dogs for years and thought it would be interesting to see the difference between a "grade" dog and a "registered" one, and I have to concede, there is a difference.

When a grade dog piddles on the floor, he often acts somewhat ashamed of himself and tends to cower and slink around afterwards.

Not so with Reuben. He braces himself on all four feet, shuts his eyes, and squeezes it off, grinning with satisfaction. Then he trots right through the puddle and comes over to you begging for a compliment. I wouldn't mind cracking him with a broom

There's a Difference Between "Registered" and "Grade" Pups

once in awhile, but when I remember what I paid for him I soon get over it.

I like the idea of owning registered animals, mainly because talking pedigrees is fun and you don't have to know much about them to become a self-proclaimed expert.

Take horses for instance. Every serious horseman has a preference or disdain for bloodlines. Horses are bred for a variety of purposes, so bloodlines are very diverse. The only breed of horses I am very familiar with is Quarter Horses. They are bred for anything from racing to cutting to reining, or for many other needs.

To talk pedigrees for pleasure, merely find out how your horses are bred and become rabid fans of that particular bloodline. Later on you can find out what type of bloodline your neighbor prefers and develop a disdain for that particular type. From that point on, you and your neighbor can argue happily for hours any time you bring up the topic. (Don't laugh. John Deere, Chevrolet, Case, and Ford fanatics, etc., have had the same mindless arguments since they were invented.)

It gives me some real pleasure knowing I have a "papered" dog, but I am having trouble talking pedigrees with my neighbors.

I have one neighbor who just bought a "grade" pup of the same breed. He calls him Woodrow. I brought Reuben over to show him one day. We watched the two pups wrestling on the floor.

"My dog is registered," I casually mentioned, barely concealing my pride.

"Oh," he said.

"Aren't you impressed?" I asked incredulously.

"Well maybe, maybe not," he replied. "What can Reuben do that Woodrow can't?"

There's a Difference Between "Registered" and "Grade" Pups

"It's not what he can do now," I explained. "The important thing is he has the bloodlines to excel in the future."

My neighbor, still unimpressed, asked what Reuben has done so far to distinguish himself.

"Well, so far," I explained, "he just dumps and pees on the floor, chews on the furniture, runs off with my socks and likes to be petted."

"So does Woodrow," he said smugly.

Some folks just don't get it!

Up Sims Creek

By: Rod Nelson

Bull Sales Provide Some of the Best Eatin' Around

Times are tough here at Sims. I've been working on income taxes. Well, not really working on the tax forms, but I am doing my 1995 record book. I started out thinking I was caught up through May, but I only had three months done. I just hung in there 'til I finished it up. Our gross income looked pretty fair until I deducted the borrowed money. I dread the thought of going in to see my tax man. He's a decent guy, but somewhat emotional and I think he feels bad for me.

This cattle market is really the pits. Looks like the only way I'll get through the spring is to attend lots of bull sales. I don't really need any bulls. I'm mainly in it for the free lunch. Gas isn't so much of an item if you can bum a ride there with someone. It's better if I can ride with someone else anyway, as it is easier to show up on time. I've missed some good feeds due to a late start with a rough running vehicle.

One of my favorite sales is Petersons' at Firesteel, SD. They put on a darn good feed and leave everything out 'til the sale is over. They don't do much bragging about their cattle either, which allows a fella to really study the cookie and bar pans.

I've been to Lelands' sale a few times but never made it in time for the noon meal. I've noticed however, if you hang around 'til long after the sale, they'll give you a dandy supper.

I saw Luella at Foresters' sale the other day and she promised to save a hot plate for me this year, no matter what time I show up. By the way Kenny, thanks alot!

For the serious eater, it is hard to beat the Leachman sale in Billings. Billings is a long way off, but when you figure you can graze steady for several days straight from morning until night you have to give it some considerations. I sometimes get so filled up at Leachmans' that I watch part of the sale. I like to bid on the bulls if I have really had time to study them. I like to pick out the very best bulls, and knowing that they will bring $20,000 or so, I like to run them up a little. It makes the missus feel like I just haven't been wasting time, running around to sales.

Bull Sales Provide Some of the Best Eatin' Around

She met me at the door the last time I got home. "How was the sale?" she asked.

"Well, OK, but I couldn't quite afford the one I wanted."

"How much did you bid?"

"I went to $13,500 and I just couldn't see going any more."

"Thirteen-five!" she gasped, "What did he sell for?"

At that point, even if the bull brought $20,000, it's best to just let her think he sold on the next bid. Women really like it if you stop in time.

You really have to bid now and then or they start to think you're a free-loader or something. It's always best to bid on the top end, too.

A friend once asked me to buy him a cheap bull at a sale he couldn't attend. I put in the opening bid on a lot of bulls, and bid on most of the bottom end. It got so that every time they ran a bull in that looked like "Yassir Arafat," all the ringmen looked at me.

When I finally got one bought, the auctioneer stopped the sale and led a round of applause. I'm still waiting for a chance to get even.

I had a lot better experience at a different sale once. I was in a feisty mood and really got active. I ran three of their best bulls right to the second to the last bid.

When the sale was over the sellers came running. Expressing sincere remorse that I hadn't been successful, they pounded me on the back and thanked me for coming. I have gotten a sale catalog from them ever since.

This time of the year you can eat at bull sales most days of the week. It's a good thing as there aren't many weddings in February and March.

Happy eating and cautious bidding!!

Up Sims Creek

By: Rod Nelson

Red Angus is One of the Most Boring Breeds of Cattle

Times are tough here at Sims. The missus thought she had one of those "near death" experiences the other night. She saw the white light and everything. Turns out it was just me walking around with no shirt on.

I had to take a heifer to the vet to get a calf out a few days ago. It's the first time I've had a calving problem with heifers since I started raising Red Angus cattle. I was beginning to think nothing goes wrong with these cattle.

The vet managed to deliver the dead calf without doing a caesarean section.

In fact, he paused and thought awhile and said, "Gosh, I can't remember for sure if I've ever done a caesarean on a Red Angus heifer." Then he added, "I hate Red Angus cattle."

I suppose with calving being copacetic for years it's about time something went wrong.

Back when I had a more eclectic cowherd it was a lot more interesting around here. After years of indiscriminate crossbreeding, calving got to be quite a challenge and I had a lot more to talk about. It used to be fun when a neighbor would swing in the yard for something. We'd visit awhile, then I'd say, "Hey, come on up to the barn, I've got a new calf to show you."

"Wow," the neighbor might say, "What a calf! His legs look like fenceposts. How much does he weigh?"

"About 148 pounds," I'd reply with a bit of pride.

"He sure is some calf," the neighbor would probably say. He'd then add, "How is the cow? Is she dead too?"

"Naw," I'd say, "just paralyzed. But I think she'll be up in a week or two. Sure hope

Red Angus is One of the Most Boring Breeds of Cattle

so, every live calf she's had has been real heavy in the fall."

The disposition of these cattle is less than interesting, too. They just sort of stand around and don't get very excited. I used to look out the window once in awhile and watch the missus sprinting across the pasture like "Flo Jo" with some irate cow in pursuit. It was a good way to measure her level of physical fitness. I couldn't really tell you what kind of shape she is in any more.

Another drawback of these cattle is that they are costlier to feed. I used to get some fairly cheap gains when my cattle grazed the neighbor's CRP. But these cattle don't want to crawl fences, even though my neighbor with the CRP is a lousy fencer.

My weaning weights are close, but not quite as high as I used to have, although I usually have a few extra calves to sell and they often sell for a little extra.

So here I sit with the best of saddle horses I have ever owned and they stand around like a bunch of Maytag repairmen.

I used to have all kinds of reasons to run a cow in; there were calving problems, bad eyes, prolapses, bad bags, calves too ignorant to suck, and so on. Nowadays about the only excuse to bring one into the barn is bad weather, and no one wants that.

Red Angus has to be one of the most boring breeds of cattle I have ever handled. I can't figure out why I like them so much. The missus really loves them!

I have some registered cattle and keep a few bulls, but they are hard for me to sell. There just isn't much I can say about them.

Up Sims Creek

By: Rod Nelson

There's No Thrill in Abusing Defenseless, Dumb Animals

Times are so tough here at Sims that the only flimsy things the missus gets from me are excuses.

Well, spring is here and the prairie is coming alive once more. Most people are into calving by now so it seems appropriate to pause and reflect a bit on issues concerning abuse to dumb animals.

Take the case of Joe and Don. These fellas were calving some cows a couple of years ago. Several cows in the herd were a little on the "hot" side, so Joe felt he needed to pack a long, heavy, fiberglass stick for a weapon in case he was attacked.

A particularly mean cow had just calved, but by using some teamwork, the boys managed to get a tag on the new baby and got away with no problems.

They then proceeded to mosey around the cowherd on foot, no doubt giving themselves some impressive accolades on how clever they were to get the tag on that new calf without getting freight-trained. At any rate, they were so engrossed in their conversation that before they knew it they had made a full circle and blundered right back almost on top of the same protective mama.

To say the old girl was less than amused would be a gross understatement. Only someone who has calved out really hot cows, or perhaps rodeo clowns and Cape Buffalo hunters, can really understand the feeling of being charged by a really ticked-off cow!

Joe, being fairly intelligent, immediately realized they were in trouble, but decided to hold his ground. I'm not sure if Joe was brave or just practical-minded enough to realize he couldn't outrun her. At any rate, he gave absolutely no consideration to the cow's welfare and drew his stick back and swung.

There's No Thrill in Abusing Defenseless, Dumb Animals

It was a classic Babe Ruth-type swing, with the follow-through typical of Mike Tyson. The stick cracked as it made contact and bit a nasty dent in the tender tissue from just below the nose to over the teeth and back on the cheekbone.

One might surmise that the only way Joe could have been more satisfied with this swing, would be if he had hit the cow instead of Don.

Don went down like the price of feeder cattle in 1996.

Joe decided he would then try to out-run the cow.

Don, no doubt, wished Joe would have watched where he was going instead of looking back at the cow. Don was frantically trying to get up when Joe tripped and fell on top of him, wrenching away what little breath he had left.

The cow stopped at the feet of the hapless duo and surveyed the situation.

We'll never know if the cow simply sensed there was too little of a challenge here or perhaps she felt a twinge of remorse about attacking poor defenseless animals. At any rate, she spun around on her heels and trotted back to her calf.

Up Sims Creek

By: Rod Nelson

My Ski Slope Apparel Not Quite the Same as Jet-Setters'

Times are really tough here at Sims. This winter is really getting long. It would have been a lot worse though if we hadn't finally gotten that week of Indian summer in March.

I managed to get a little break a couple weeks ago when I had occasion to spend a couple days in Squaw Valley, CA.

When I landed at the Reno airport, the first thing I noticed were the slot machines. They reminded me instantly of the gamble I was taking by leaving home during calving. I felt no compulsion to drop coins in the machines, my gamble on the weather was enough.

I had most of the next day to kill and as my host provided me with free ski rentals and lift tickets I thought I'd give it a try. I am not an accomplished skier, but since I had conquered most of the major slopes in North Dakota back in the '70s, I felt confident I would fit in well with the Jet Set at Squaw Valley.

I figured I had packed all the ski clothing I needed, but discovered I'd neglected to bring a cap. After checking prices at the ski shops, I casually strolled down the road a bit, hoping to stumble into a KMart. No such luck. Despite better sense, I returned to the trendy shops at the resort and purchased the most expensive, ugly cap I've ever owned.

The folks at the rental shop soon had me outfitted with all the proper equipment, and I soon found myself in the gondola heading to the top of the mountain. It was an eerie feeling swinging in a box suspended on a cable so high up in the air. My mouth was dry, stomach in knots, and I was close to losing bladder control – much the same feeling I get when I visit my loan officer.

I felt much better when we got off the thing at the top of the mountain. The

My Ski Slope Apparel Not Quite the Same as Jet-Setters'

weather calmed me down a lot. The winds were tremendous up there. Snow and chunks of fine ice pounded and bit you like shrapnel. It reminded me of North Dakota. Many people elected to take the gondola back down rather than face the weather.

The weather was the only thing that hadn't bothered me so far, so I followed some skiers who seemed to know their way around and managed to ski to a place about halfway down the mountain where the weather was better and chair lifts were operating.

I scanned the crowds as I waited for the chair lift. I noticed everyone else had kind of an "Eddie Bauer" look. I suddenly realized that I was the only one there who wouldn't have looked out of place in a sale barn.

I slid into the chair with a nice looking older woman. I figured she wasn't much younger than me.

"Don't you wear ski goggles?" she asked.

"No," I said. "I just squint a lot."

I complemented her on her beautiful ski outfit.

"Thank you," she replied curtly, adding that she shopped a lot at L.L. Bean for her outdoor clothes. I told her where I bought my Wranglers and was stunned to learn she had never even heard of Sandvigs.

Trying to make conversation, I mentioned her nice gloves.

"Oh," she said. "These are 'Hot Fingers' that I got at the lodge."

"Mine are 'Wells Lamont' that I bought at Cenex," I replied lamely.

It was a long ride up on the lift. Still trying to make some conversation I told her

My Ski Slope Apparel Not Quite the Same as Jet-Setters'

she sure smelled nice.

"I'm wearing 'Obsession by Calvin Klein'," she said, then added, "you have kind of an exotic aroma yourself. What is it?"

I was puzzled for a bit, then sniffed my "Handy Andys" and told her I thought it was a mixture of "Warbex" and horse manure.

"Warbex?" she said.

"Yeah, I use it to kill grubs and lice."

About that time we reached the top and I never saw her again.

I also went swimming in a heated outside pool surrounded by snowbanks and did the hot tub thing as well.

I really wasn't impressed with much of anything at the resort. Ranchers can't enjoy much of anything when they are away from home at calving time.

Up Sims Creek

By: Rod Nelson

In This Cattle Market, Ranching is Becoming More Like a Hobby

Times are tough here at Sims. If you don't believe me just check the cattle market.

There are many things that a rancher's fortune depends on, like the weather, the market, disease problems, etc. This market, like everything else, is just something we'll have to endure. Most of us on the northern prairie have always taken pride in the hardships we've had to face at one time or another and these challenges and trials have given us lots to talk about.

Take 1936, for example. Some people never talked about much of anything else. 1936 was a conversational gold mine. 60 degrees below zero – 120 degrees above, no rain, and all agricultural products practically worthless. It was a grand year to have survived. Notable times since then have been the drought of '61, blizzards of '66 and '75, cattle market crash of '74, or in some areas the flooding of recent years. Few can tell you about great years, many know about the tough times. Salty old ranchers and farmers recall those times with pride, secure in the knowledge that they were durable enough to make it.

These old timers also are proud of the rugged lifestyle they had. They like to tell you how they never had a vacation or wasted any time with hobbies.

To the best of my understanding, a hobby is something one does outside of his regular occupation for fun or relaxation.

At times in my life when asked what my hobbies were I suppose I've mentioned training colts and writing poetry. The other day I was reflecting a bit on my life and it struck me that breaking colts and writing poems have consistently made me a few bucks. My part-time brand inspection job makes me a few bucks.

It hit me like a thunderbolt when I realized that at the current cattle market, I am ranching for a hobby!

In This Cattle Market, Ranching is Becoming More Like a Hobby

This creates a bit of a dilemma, as I have often heard people ridiculed for wasting too much time on hobbies. I don't mind ranching for a hobby so much as the fact that it takes up so darn much time. I have often had to ride my colts before breakfast so I had all day to build fences, do some farming, or bale some hay. How am I going to justify putting off writing poems any more, just to waste time on some hobby like hauling manure?

On the bright side, things should be a lot more fun from now on. Since I am now a hobby rancher, all of those chores will become fun and relaxin'!

At long last, I'll enjoy fixing machinery. The thought of rolling around in the dirt and grease used to strike terror in me, but now what a pleasure it will be to thrash around under a worn-out piece of haying equipment, with chaff running down my neck, oil dripping in my eyes, and leaving assorted chunks of meat and hide on sharp corners every time my crescent wrench slips.

It's mighty comforting to know that freezing on my open air loader tractor is now fun and relaxing. I used to wonder why people would pay good money to freeze on a snowmobile all winter. Now they may ask the same of me.

Wow! The possibilities out there are almost endless for zest and merriment. Every time I have to work on a cow that hasn't cleaned, clean out a grain bin when it is 100 degrees, or patch up a section of fence the bulls tore down, I can remind myself of all the fun I am having.

This cattle market shows no signs of improving anytime soon.

It's going to be lots of fun ranching for a hobby. Sure hope I can afford it!

Up Sims Creek

By: Rod Nelson

Spring Cleanup On the Ranch Means Clearing the Bones

Times are tough here at Sims. It must be bad, as I'm getting bald and gray at the same time. I really wish I could afford a toupee. That's probably a frivolous idea, but maybe I could justify it if I could get one with built-in ear flaps.

I hate these late springs when a fella still needs a winter cap in May. I sure hope spring gets here before the days start getting shorter. That is only about six weeks away.

Oh, it's coming I guess. The signs of spring are here again. I hear meadowlarks now every day. The meadowlark must have quite a good attitude to fly up on a snow-covered fencepost and sing his heart out to such a small and apathetic audience as you find on blustery spring days.

Birds are probably one of the best signs of spring, along with the dead calves lying by the barn, the deeply rutted driveway, and the muddy overshoes piled by the front door. Another good sign is when the missus won't let you in the house 'til you've stripped down to your shorts on the porch.

Birds though, really mean spring. Many of them, like robins, just seem to show up. You look out the window one day and there they are!

Geese let us know they're back. You hear them first and scan the sky until you finally see the big V heading North. They seem to have a deadline to make and move fast and deliberately to their goal.

My favorite is the sandhill crane. I couldn't begin to describe the sound they make, but I like it a lot. You always hear them long before you see them. Finally, there they are – way, way up – usually circling. They make the same trip as everyone else but always seem to have time enough to slow up, look the country over and enjoy the trip.

Spring Cleanup On the Ranch Means Clearing the Bones

Another undeniable sign of spring is the inevitable yard cleanup. For lots of people that would mean raking leaves, tilling flower beds and gardens and things of this sort. In ranch country, however, there is a critical first step in yard cleanup.

If you have ever read any pioneer history books you have no doubt seen the classic photos of a haggard looking pioneer couple with a scrawny team of oxen pulling a heaping load of buffalo bones. Scratch the team of oxen and you have a typical image of spring cleanup in Sims. I wish our dogs would start collecting arrowheads or something, but they are big into bones. You have to pick them up as they're just too darn hard on lawn mowers. If they would ever invent a lawnmower that would cut grass and turn bones to dust, ranch wives would kill for them.

Now, if you drive through the city in the spring you will see delicate ladies with gardening gloves, working with gaily painted carts filled with gardening tools. But, if you drive on out to ranch country you will see bare-handed women walking along dragging a whole cow leg with one hand, picking up various pieces of bones and cow hide with the other. The wheelbarrow she managed to sneak away from the barn will be squatting low from the load she has piled on it. I have always wondered where the missus goes with the bones. Only her and the dogs know for sure.

My mother had the same problem. I can remember her complaining about all the bones when the snow melted. My dad, eyeing a couple sons he didn't think were working hard enough, would comment, "I like those bones lying around. It shows that there was once life on this ranch!"

Spring cleanup to my dad meant only one thing. FIRE! Dad was raised a farmer and never got over the pyromania that farmers are born with. A carry-over from the days when they had to burn the thistles perhaps. Anyway, when I was a kid, if you saw lots of billowing smoke at the ranch, you knew dad was doing his part of spring

Spring Cleanup On the Ranch Means Clearing the Bones

cleanup. He always thought it was foolish to rake anything you could burn.

A good cleanup job to dad meant that the fire was good enough so that he just barely managed to save the buildings. And if you didn't manage to burn up a few trees and singe the dog you weren't really trying. Mom had two spruce trees she had planted in the yard. They had a tough time growing and looked pretty ragged until one spring dad burned one of them almost completely up. It recovered, and then proceeded to grow at twice the rate of the other one. After that, if anyone discussed raising evergreens, Dad would perk up and explain the benefits of his fire treatment.

Dad was a wonderful firefighter. He could put out more fire with a shovel and a denim shirt than most rural fire departments could handle with a $100,000 truck and a crew. He should have been good. He set enough of them!

Up Sims Creek

By: Rod Nelson

Oprah's Spree on BSE (Bovine Spongiform Encephalopathy)

Times are tough here at Sims. The cattle market is so poor I have to pinch pennies instead of the missus.

I've been hearing a lot about the video gambling issue on the radio lately. Advocates talk about all the money this will generate for North Dakota. Opponents, like former governor Art Link, have lots of good reasons why it shouldn't be allowed. I'm going to side with Art. I can't see why anyone who farms or ranches should need a machine for gambling.

There are countless ways we gamble every day. Most of us are still gambling that the weather will warm up before fall, although we are losing a little hope. Many of us gamble that our banker has a tiny shred of compassion somewhere in his heart. We could make countless bets with ourselves that wouldn't cost us a cent. The poorest bet we could make is that we could make some money by playing some gambling machine. We all know that they are set to make money for the house. You can't possibly beat them.

Others, better informed, could find many reasons for not allowing gambling. All I know is people who cannot afford to lose will be losing. These people will squander money they could use to buy things like beef for their family. I am going to vote against expanding gambling. Beef producers have enough problems as it is . . . like Oprah's show.

Oprah's Spree on BSE
(Bovine Spongiform Encephalopathy)

Did you see Oprah on TV?
Distorting facts of BSE.

Oprah's Spree on BSE (Bovine Spongiform Encephalopathy)

The guests she's had for years, not weeks,
Were kinky folks, like sex change freaks.

But then one day, we don't know why,
Her "weirdo well" I guess ran dry.

So Oprah then up and invites
A champion of animal rights.

He made this claim we could with ease,
Contract this deadly brain disease.

Yes, he said, 'twas his belief,
It could be spread by eating beef.

Now BSE I do not fear.
It's never been reported here.

But listen folks in the USA
A greater danger exists today!

A virus? Yes, a malady
Transmits en-ceph-alop-athy.

This thing has spread across the nation,
Creating brain degeneration.

The cause, oh yes, as bright ones know,
Is watching trash, like Oprah's show!

Up Sims Creek

By: Rod Nelson

Impressive Structures Give New Meaning to Old Saying

Times are tough here at Sims. If summer is as late as spring, it will be winter before fall.

It looks like we won't be able to have much of a vacation this summer due to the sorry cattle market. Disney World and Disney Land are unlikely. The Grand Canyon won't be possible. The Rocky Mountains won't see us either.

It looks like the only vacation for us this summer will be in good old North Dakota. That is not to say that North Dakota doesn't have some interesting places to visit. I have always wanted to see the reconstructed Fort Union. With so much historical value, I think a short trip there would be very rewarding. All of us have had a chance to tour the Custer House at Fort Lincoln, and found the tour pleasant as well as informative.

There are a number of state parks worth visiting, but some of the smaller tourist draws like the David Thompson Memorial at Verendrye or the Sondre Norheim grave at Denbigh, might be fun as well.

The trouble with most of these things is that it would take more than a tank of gas to get there, which would put us a bit over budget.

The good news is that quite possibly the best tourist draw in North Dakota is under construction a few miles from here and is nearing completion. I am talking, of course, about the new toilets they are building on the sides of I-94 a few miles west of New Salem.

I understand that the reconstruction of Fort Union cost around $4 million, largely due to archaeology work that needed to be done there. I don't know how many people visit there, but it must be considerable.

Impressive Structures Give New Meaning to Old Saying

The Custer house, reconstructed with about $500,000 of private funds, has 30,000-50,000 visitors per year who pay a small fee to see it.

Can you imagine how many people will come to North Dakota to see our new $800,000 toilets? Yes, not one, but two $800,000 outhouses. They are impressive structures giving meaning to the old saying, "Built like a brick outhouse," or something like that.

I have traveled I-94 from Chicago to Seattle and have seen nothing to rival them. We can truly be proud. No doubt, people traveling through Minnesota and Montana will push on regardless of personal discomfort just so they can relieve themselves in North Dakota, and, believe me, after bouncing across that much rough concrete they will be ready to stop.

It will be fun having a real tourist trap so close to home. We can force-feed the kids lots of liquids and when the need arises we can be at the rest area in 10 minutes. After reading the latest graffiti and checking out the most recent vandalism, we can cruise a few more miles to Glen Ullin, toss down a few sodas and hit the other one on the way home.

No doubt many of North Dakota's homeless will be staying in these new heated back houses. In fact, some homeless folks may move to North Dakota just to "Hole Up" there.

Through the years I have watched many people hanging gamely onto their hats as they struggled to get from their cars to the toilets during periods of gale force winds.

It's comforting to have the knowledge that even tho' these people may not think North Dakota is a good place to visit, it will certainly be a great place to "go"!!

Up Sims Creek

By: Rod Nelson

To Weed Trees You First Have to Find the Trees

Things are picking up here at Sims. The cows are on grass and there's nothing left in the corrals to feed. It is always nice to have that little gap between feeding hay and making the stuff.

I finished the yearly ritual of tree planting just a couple days ago. If one enjoys planting trees, it's hard to beat Western North Dakota. You don't need to go to a lot of preparation to get the land ready to plant trees because most of the time you can plant them on the same ground year after year. The good news is you don't have to blame yourself for the death of last year's crop. Nature usually helps us out. Drought, grasshoppers, stampedes and frost generally take their toll, however if you don't mind blaming yourself you can admit weeds were a factor.

Weeding and hoeing trees is a tough job unless you have a wife that is addicted to such labor. It is so hard to find the time to get out there when you should be out there. Actually I think you'd have to be a little lazy to hoe trees right on time. Hoeing trees when the weeds are barely out of the ground presents a very small challenge.

In the interest of physical fitness I usually wait until the weed stems are at least an inch thick. This makes for great aerobic exercise, but is a little tough on hoes. Many Far East countries have received a sound cursing from me when I am hoeing. A few licks and the modern hoes straighten right out. The last hoe I bought folded up in a "V" within a few minutes. I sure wish I could buy a quality American-made hoe but I don't know where to find one.

Actually I get by fairly well with a machete and my ax. With such tools you can almost always find your way back out of the tree patch in time for lunch.

One of the hardest things about hoeing trees is getting my kids out there to help.

"Hey kids, I think it's time we do some bonding."

"Oh no, not hoeing!" they scream.

To Weed Trees You First Have to Find the Trees

Usually by the time I have leg irons on one of them, the second one will come along without much protest.

Perhaps the biggest challenge is finding the trees. One person usually takes the lead and after traveling the approximate distance, drops to his knees and starts parting the weeds. If the search is productive he remains on the spot until the rest of the crew arrives. Sometimes the tree is still alive. If this is the case we try pulling enough weeds around the trees so we can clearly see the tree when we hoe. This is a good theory, but the tree usually suffers a fatal swipe anyway.

If the tree is already dead we try to work up the ground a bit in that spot so we can come back and spade in a replacement. The main thing is to hoe or pull enough weeds around the trees so one can detect the rows from a tractor seat. If I can clearly see the rows I seem to kill fewer trees with the cultivator.

I buy lots of replacement trees every year. The Morton County SCS usually has leftover trees we can buy for 50 cents each. Others I buy direct from the Towner nursery. I prefer those I get from Morton County. I don't have to watch them die. They are usually dead when I buy them. It perhaps isn't fair to say that. The problem is that those trees usually get planted pretty late and are more exposed to heat stress and drought.

I wonder how many thousands of trees I have planted here at Sims in the last 12 years.

I do have three rows of evergreens along my driveway that are really nice. We have invested a lot of sweat in those trees, but being practical-minded I keep waiting for some disaster to wipe them out. If you have ever had 10-year-old trees die you can appreciate those trees that were considerate enough to croak the first year.

Up Sims Creek

By: Rod Nelson

Prairie Areas Offer Beautiful "Treeless" View

Times are great here at Sims. I really enjoyed spring and so did lots of other people, since it happened to fall on a weekend this year.

Summer seems to be here in full force. Very hot and ample supplies of flies and bugs. Pretty fair moisture here at Sims, but some rain sure wouldn't hurt. Everything is still pretty green and there is lots of grass.

I remember asking my dad once what his favorite color was. "Green," he said, "but only on grass."

Most of us prairie dwellers have heard negative comments so often about the prairie from our city cousins that we often fail to see the beauty of it ourselves.

The average traveler through prairie areas often makes a statement like, "How can you stand it out here?" or "I have never seen such god-forsaken country in my life." Such comments are inevitably followed by references to the lack of trees in this country. Seems like travelers think trees are really something to look at.

I once drove east through northern Minnesota, Wisconsin, and the U.P. on through Ontario and clear to the coast through New York, Vermont, New Hampshire, and Maine. I must say I saw lots of trees but failed to see much glamour in them. Rarely could you see farther than the edge of the ditch.

We know trees are overrated but we still stand by and let others berate the prairie with their insensitive comments about the lack of trees.

Perhaps that is why we feel compelled to try and raise as many trees as we can.

In my case I dream of having some place where I can stand out of the wind or more importantly, create a place where my livestock can stand out of the wind.

Prairie Areas Offer Beautiful "Treeless" View

Nearly everyone can appreciate the comfort and shelter of trees but we sure have developed some funny attitudes about trees.

When planting trees we almost always plant them too thick, with the idea of thinning them later. This is a great idea but how many people have ever thinned out a row of trees? A person could be forgiven by his neighbors for a variety of crimes, but never for cutting down a tree. Even if we have a tree growing right in the way we can't bear to cut it down. People would rather see a new highway cut through a cemetery than ruin a lone cottonwood standing out on the prairie.

People also have no patience when planting trees. No one wants to wait for a tree to grow. People still plant Siberian Elms because they are fast growing.

Face it folks, a Siberian Elm is about as attractive as a cat with distemper. Nothing has spoiled the looks of the prairie more than the one-row belts of Siberian Elms. The next time you see a one-row belt of these elms, just imagine how much better the country would look like if it was pure grass. We can all appreciate the beautiful shelter belts of various trees that people have worked so hard to grow, but have you ever seen a planted tree that looked half as good as trees that grow naturally along rivers and streams?

The finest straight rows of spruce or pines can't compare with the looks of natural groves growing in draws or coulees.

I love the looks of northeast North Dakota where the prairie intermingles with the natural forests of the hills. I actually can't find any areas of the state that I don't enjoy, but I get a real special feeling when I find a spot like the one heading north from Ruso to Velva, when all of a sudden the prairie just busts open and lets you look at about a zillion acres all at once.

Prairie Areas Offer Beautiful "Treeless" View

Other great open prairie areas can be found here and there. Drive west from Bottineau to Montana. Pay attention and every now and then you will still find a place where the view is similar to what the pioneers wrote about.

Every time I drive through the Red River Valley I try to find a spot where the view is uninterrupted, but usually there are trees in the way.

I make no apologies for the treelessness of North Dakota. I can always find lots of things to look at when driving through the prairie.

I just came back from Rapid City. In parts of western South Dakota there are still some areas that no one has tried to improve. Not a tree, building, or some powerline in sight. With recent rains it was all green and pretty.

Sure hope it rains here soon at Sims. The trees I planted this spring could sure use it!

Up Sims Creek

By: Rod Nelson

Ranch Wives Really Love – and Appreciate – New Lawn Mowers

Times are tough here at Sims. I bought a new haying tractor and felt I was finally making progress until some insensitive individual mentioned that it was almost 40 years old.

I must be getting old. It seems like only yesterday that the "720" was invented. It is still a nice tractor – comfortable, good power steering, good hydraulics, excellent visibility. However, it would be nice if that little starting engine worked, but I really don't need it. We have an excellent selection of hills in the Sims area, perfect for starting tractors.

Another nice feature of this tractor is a nice box someone built on the front. I suppose it was built for carrying the occasional rock off the field, but it also is a nice place to carry a chain in case you have to park on the level.

Once you get one of those things started, you can leave them running without worrying much about the greenhouse effect, as they run so efficiently. I filled this one plumb full the first day and noticed a severe leak in the fuel tank. We mowed with it for two hours and then parked it for the night. The next morning I noticed the drip was still steady, but the tank was still full. Lucky we mowed a couple hours or it might have run over!

I've kind of been in a machinery buying mood lately. At the risk of spoiling the missus I bought her a new mower the other day. It took considerable time and effort before I finally found the proper model. It is getting harder and harder to find a $100 mower these days. Most of the economy mowers are costing at least $130 or more.

Yard mowing is considerably different here in the Sims area than it is in the Red River Valley. I have noticed the neatly manicured, fertilized and level farm yards in eastern North Dakota. At times I have seen the machines that groom these yards.

Ranch Wives Really Love – and Appreciate – New Lawn Mowers

They must cost thousands of dollars and they are often piloted by men.

I think too much of the missus to risk spoiling her like that! Why would I deprive her of all of that beneficial aerobic exercise, besides, the mechanical knowledge she has gained has been invaluable.

I remember the first mower I bought her right after we were married. I parked it in the back yard to surprise her. I'll never forget her words when she found it: "Honey, would you please haul this junk away to the pit?"

"That is not junk, my dear," I replied. "This baby is your new mower. You do know what a mower is, don't you?"

"Of course," she said, "Daddy had one, but his had paint and four wheels."

"Well, if it will make you fell any better, Hon, this one used to be red and if you lift up on one handle and push down on the other it'll mow just dandy, besides, you can tell your friends I bought you a three-wheeler."

I remember back then how she would often ask me to help her start it. I've never cared much for starting lawn mowers. After about 65 pulls on the starting cord my patience would grow so thin that the missus would volunteer to take over. Wasn't long 'til she could start most any mower.

She must have found and read an owner's manual somewhere as well. Sometimes I see her fiddling with the spark plug, blowing on the gas line or oiling that sponge looking thing. She won't even let me touch the mowers anymore.

Having her own machinery has also taught her a lot about maintenance. After a bunch of horses chewed off all the wires on her last mower, she has really gotten good about keeping it locked up in the garage. She got it running again, but never

Ranch Wives Really Love – and Appreciate – New Lawn Mowers

had much control over the throttle after that.

She still relies on me for the occasional blade sharpening, although it is quite a challenge to sharpen a ranch wife's mower. For some reason, ranch women develop a casual attitude about mowing into rocks and scrap iron, which gives the blade the appearance of the teeth in a 17-year-old cow.

Ranch wives really love new mowers. It was almost embarrassing to see her break into tears, hug my legs and kiss my feet when she saw the brand new 20-inch 3.5 hp mower. It was quite a shock to her system. I won't be buying any new ones for quite a spell. It's just too hard on her!

Up Sims Creek

By: Rod Nelson

Olympic Events Have Nothing Over Ranching Feats

Times are tough here at Sims. The Olympics only come once every four years and I really can't enjoy them. No, it's not that I don't have time. It doesn't bother me to take a little time to watch them, it's just that for me it's kind of a "been there, done that," sort of thing.

For instance, take any of those events where men are twisting and spinning high in the air. During my long and colorful career as a bronc rider, I have made all of these moves.

During gymnastics competition, I notice that to achieve a high score, the competitor must land squarely on both feet and not take an additional step or sit down. You don't need to be a rocket scientist to realize that would do irreparable damage to your knees.

In the spirit of body conservation, most of my landings were head first. In later years, after age 40, my technique changed to a full reclining position landing, so all parts of the spine and the back of the legs and head took part of the blow. This is somewhat less spectacular than the one-point head landing, but you deserve 10 points just for getting back up on your feet. Either way, your knees are spared.

The high hurdles are impressive for some, but I've seen equal or greater feats from the missus during calving time. Her speed is even more impressive when you consider the four-buckle overshoes on her feet and the newborn calf in her arms.

I am truly impressed with that little Turkish gold metal weightlifter who lifts three times his weight, and smokes 50 cigarettes a day. Must be a terrific feeling to have muscle and bad breath at the same time.

I think the swimming events are a tad too easy. I doubt if it would be to hard swimming around practically naked like these Olympic swimmers do. Being a rancher I have had little time during the hot months for leisure swimming activities.

Olympic Events Have Nothing Over Ranching Feats

My best, and most important swimming was done wearing a parka and ice skates. I'm not sure what type of stroke I used, but let me assure you, it was rapid.

Another advantage of these Olympians is that they are all skinny. What is the big deal about thin people being fast? Think how much more impressive it would be if they used people about 40 pounds overweight like the average North Dakotan.

Can you imagine how crowds would hold their breath to see Roseanne on the balance beam or Al Roker trying to nail a landing off the high bar?

The only real athlete in my family is my big brother Orrin.

Early in 1963, President Kennedy dug up some old Marine regulation that stated that a Marine should be able to move 50 miles on foot in one day. This started a rage across the nation of people attempting to run 50 miles and could very well have been the start of the big modern super marathons.

Big brother and some other high school seniors and juniors had someone haul them 50 miles from Towner to a point south of Minot and drop them off. This was right after school on a Friday night, February 16, 1963, so I assume he was wearing something a little more substantial than running briefs and a tee shirt.

Twelve hours later, at 6 a.m. Saturday, he trotted into Towner. One other boy made it in later.

Thirty-three years ago Reebok and Nike weren't heard of. Most of the guys had foot problems. Perhaps his big advantage was the fact that he was wearing the most expensive footwear of the group – Hyer Cowboy Boots. (No kiddin'!) The heels and soles were pretty much gone after 50 miles of pavement.

I believe he did write to the Hyer Boot Company hoping to get a new pair for his

Olympic Events Have Nothing Over Ranching Feats

feat and I believe they said, "Congratulations."

The run did give him some notoriety, as he made the front page of the Mouse River Farmers Press.

Well, enough on athletics, I'm heading out to the shop to pump some real iron.

Up Sims Creek

8-16-96
Col. 31

By: Rod Nelson

The "Composite Cowdog" is Indeed a Breathtaking Sight

Times have been tough here at Sims. I'll admit there were days when my life seemed to amount to nothing. I haven't felt like I really needed a big place in history, but one can't help but wish that something you have done, invented, or developed for the benefit of mankind, would be recognized by future generations.

People like Benjamin Franklin, Thomas Edison, Jonas Salk, and Sondre Norheim will never be forgotten for their contributions to society.

Since I have always been involved with livestock it is logical that my contribution to humanity would be somewhere in agriculture.

I have always been intrigued with geneticists who have developed new breeds of cattle and horses, and like many in the cattle industry, I have observed with interest the development of "composites" in the last years. "Composites," to the uninformed, are mixtures of several breeds. Cattle composites supposedly retain much heterosis, thereby are reportedly superior for growth as well as other desirable traits.

It was not for selfish reasons; no, it was merely the satisfaction I had in knowing that future cattlemen would lead happier, more productive, and less stressful lives; that I began work on the development of the "composite cowdog." Finding the proper base was not easy, but several years ago blind luck led me to a place south of Wibaux, MT, where I was fortunate enough to find the perfect female pup with which to start my composite breed.

This pup, besides having a black roof in her mouth, was extraordinarily beautiful and displayed much intelligence. I was so impressed, I paid her owner twenty dollars more for her than he asked.

It soon became apparent that this Australian Shepherd/Border Collie cross was no ordinary dog. I consider myself a geneticist, not a trainer, so I was duly impressed

The "Composite Cowdog" is Indeed a Breathtaking Sight

with this dog's desire to work. To see her silky rapid movements behind a herd of cattle is breathtaking. In fact, after some sessions in which she works the hardest, I have been out of breath for quite some time.

Never a dull dog, besides cattle and horses, she also shows an active interest in coyotes and cottontails.

I never had a doubt that at some time, a proper mate for her would show up and sure enough one day I looked out the kitchen window and there he was. A mixture of Blue Heeler and Morton County Stock Special, it was apparent he possessed many desirable traits, especially the one for fertility.

This dog is so ambitious that he is not content to be a mere stay-at-home cowdog that passes away into oblivion. No, this dog has broadened his horizons by visiting many area ranches, where he not only has learned new techniques, but has been eager to pass along his knowledge as well as his genes.

July 6th will go down in history as the day the first litter of the Sims Creek Cowdog Composites were whelped.

My years of work had culminated with impressive results. Ten pups and not an ugly one in the bunch.

To properly price these pups was an agonizing decision. No doubt some will be outstanding companions as well as top cowdogs. Others in the litter will provide an instant aerobic exercise benefit, as their owners may experience an increased heart rate merely by watching them work.

I considered pricing them anywhere up to $500, but have decided to make an introductory offer of $35 for males and $40 for females.

The "Composite Cowdog" is Indeed a Breathtaking Sight

Are you a proper candidate for purchasing and owning a composite cowdog? If you epitomize the modern successful agriculturist, this dog is for you. However, if your operation is somewhat backward, let's say you don't have much for new paint around your machinery lot, you haven't retained ownership of any of your calf crops, you perhaps "heaven forbid" are satisfied with the amount of land you own or operate and haven't had a $400,000 write-down, the purchase of a composite cowdog is an affordable way to sail into the modern agriculture of the 21st century.

The pups are ready. The kids and the missus have spent countless hours gentling and giving them pre-potty training instruction as well as dreaming up various potential names for them. The pups aren't papered, but for an additional 25 bucks I am sure we can include some kind of paperwork with them.

P.S. They might work out fine as pets, too.

Up Sims Creek

By: Rod Nelson

Haying Made Good Hands, Good Workers and Big Tales

Times are tough here at Sims. I hope I get my pups sold before the grasshoppers eat them, too.

Funny how times have changed. Back when I was a kid, we used to pull into the hayfields with three tractors totaling about 90 horsepower and we just hayed in the daytime.

Modern technology has made it possible to do the same job with about triple the horsepower and now you often have to hay at night as well.

I never did get much of a kick out of haying at night. It is lonesome enough to hay in the daytime these days.

I had some clover to put up this summer and since I have now raised a suitable "crew," I put the hay basket on the old Farmhand and hooked up the mower and rake and we went haying. It's the most fun I've had in the field since I moved to Sims.

My 12-year-old son and 13-year-old daughter were good hands. It was lots of fun to wave at them and see their smiles of pride as they steered their machines across the fields. It sort of reminded me of the '60's when I was a kid.

At that time, any rancher's son who didn't have a job in the hayfield by the time he was 11 or 12 was definitely considered a wimp. There were lots of younger ones out there as well and many ranchers proudly pointed out the fact that their daughters were their best hands. The girls probably weren't the best at fixing machinery but they usually wrecked a lot less stuff than the boys did because they tended to drive the tractors in the gears that their dads told them to.

Almost all ranchers had a crew haying somewhere. The size of the crew was often determined by their religion, so it could be anywhere from three on up. The dad nearly always did the stacking and, out of necessity, was chief mechanic as well.

Haying Made Good Hands, Good Workers and Big Tales

Breakdowns were a problem, as every kid had to shut down and come over and see what was wrong. A broken sickle or a lost hitch pin could stop the whole crew. Once in a while the dad would have to make a parts run, leaving the crew out there alone. This almost always made for interesting watching. Two cylinder John Deeres and various other low horsepower tractors often set new speed records when the boss left the field.

Breaking in a new kid was relatively easy. The dad or an older brother or sister would probably make a round with the new hand and then he or she was turned loose. The last bit of advise was most often "don't hit anything."

The new hand was always obvious, as they would proudly wave to everyone driving by, oblivious to the 1/4 mile of barbed wire dragging behind their rake.

I was third in the family and since Dad already had a mower and rake operator, he had a power bullrake built and it became my machine. My bullrake, also called a sweeprake, power sweeprake, or most commonly, a bucker, was a 1947 Dodge truck turned around and run backwards.

The bucker operator was the most envied kid in the hayfield as it was by far the fastest machine. It was a lot of fun to gas the Dodge down the field and gun it in a couple tight circles close to where my older brother, green with envy, was grinding along with his mower.

Saturday night conversation in town among the kids was mostly about how much hay they put up that week, what gear they drove in, and how mad their dad got when something broke down. There was also some complaining about how hard they had to work, but the pride they had in their jobs was evident.

Lots of town kids had hayfield jobs too, so it was just a few of the rich town kids who were left out of the conversation.

Those days are fading. It's too bad. It made good hands and good workers out of lots of kids.

Up Sims Creek

By: Rod Nelson

Grasshoppers are Good Sport and a New Food Source

Times are tough here at Sims. I don't seem to get any respect. The other day I asked a nice old neighbor lady if she read my column. "Oh yes," she said, "I always read your column and then I read Val Farmer to heal up."

I heard a terrible racket in the yard a couple days ago. It sounded kinda like the flapping sound a tire makes after a blowout, mixed in with a lot of kicking sounds, punctuated with an occasional blood curdling scream. Turns out that a herd of grasshoppers had the missus down out there by the trash barrel. Good thing I hadn't sold all those composite cowdog pups yet. I sicked them on the hoppers and saved her life. It was really her own darn fault. I told her not to wear green!

I suppose the grasshoppers have been worse, but this is the toughest I've ever seen them. I have 25' high cottonwood trees with the leaves stripped clear to the top and they have killed all the trees I planted last spring, except for a few Junipers.

The hoppers really bothered me a lot when they first got bad. It was bad enough when they ate up all the grass, but when I had to start buying milk replacer for my pups 'cuz the hoppers kept sucking the mother dog dry, I thought that was going too far!

Believing that it is always best to make the most out of a bad situation, I decided to make sport out of them. The time of day is very important when using hoppers as game animals as the little grasshoppers are the first to move around each morning and the biggest ones come out last.

I used to enjoy fishing until the hoppers drank the Sims Creek dry, and not wishing to lose all my fishing skills, I have started doing a little dryland fishing right out the kitchen door. I just bait a hook with a corn cob and toss it out in the yard. They will hit the bait with amazing speed, but you don't really dare to try to crank them in until they swallow the hook.

Grasshoppers are Good Sport and a New Food Source

It is great to watch them fight and jump. Care must be taken so as not to get tangled up in the highline wires, however. I can usually have them up to the door in 15 minutes or less and then I send the missus out to stun them with a baseball bat so they don't wreck any furniture when we pull them inside.

I haven't done much catch and release as even the animal rights people don't seem to care if you kill them. This truly makes for good sport, but can only be done early in the morning when the little ones are out.

As the slightly larger ones get active, they make excellent shotgun targets. Ten gauge shotguns are the weapon of choice but 12-gauge magnums are satisfactory. You can find good pass shooting most anywhere, but for me, nothing beats the excitement of shooting over decoys. I usually save a couple small ones caught with the hook and tie them up by a hind leg. This will soon bring hordes of adults within shooting range.

Late in the afternoon, all but the most foolhardy use only center fire rifles of 30 caliber or larger. A word of caution here. Never! Never! follow a wounded grasshopper into any thick brush.

Properly prepared grasshopper makes for some mighty tasty treats. Many folks seem to enjoy the drumsticks, but I have just been saving the backstraps. Another substitute for red meat, grasshoppers that have been eating corn fields taste remarkably like chicken. Hoppers that have been feeding down in slough bottoms however, need quite a bit of seasoning as they taste more like coots. At any rate, proper field dressing and quick cooling is essential. People who have been driving around with their hoppers lashed on to the hood of their cars usually resort to grinding them up for sausage and then run around the neighborhood trying to give all their friends a couple of packages.

If you would like to get in on a grasshopper hunt you should hustle on down to

Grasshoppers are Good Sport and a New Food Source

Almont or probably most anywhere in the Morton County area. The Game and Fish Department, as of yet, hasn't required grasshopper licenses and there is no bag limit. Hunting access is easy as the hoppers have eaten up all the "No Hunting" signs.

Have a safe and happy hunt!

Up Sims Creek

By: Rod Nelson

Kaycee is a place where North Dakota means something other than "blizzard"

Things are picking up here at Sims. We got a shower of rain just in time to save our grasshoppers.

I got itchy feet a couple of weeks ago. Really felt it was time for a little vacation. I had already taken the kids up to the Interstate to see the new rest rooms and there is no way the missus can take off this time of the year with all the hay left to haul, so I decided to go by myself.

I'd heard how the rodeo at Kaycee, WY was voted the best Small PRCA Rodeo in the USA in 1995 so I decided to check it out.

Kaycee has always meant rodeo, and bronc riders, in particular. As long as I can remember, there have been prominent bronc riders from Kaycee, and if you check back you'll find that Kaycee has been producing bronc riders since the 1920s and before. There have been world champions from Kaycee and many NFR competitors, but the current PRCA rodeo is held as a memorial to Deke Latham, who was killed at age 21 just after completing his first NFR.

An added plus at Kaycee is single steer roping which is not seen in most places.

The thought of driving 500 miles to a rodeo I wasn't entered in seemed a bit strange, but I figured it would be a good weekend.

I knew I'd enjoy the drive down there. I've heard dozens of people complain about the desolate stretches of road in Wyoming, but I personally love it. If you pay attention, you can see a lot more in 10 miles of Wyoming than you can see in 100 miles of city driving.

I got to Kaycee Friday afternoon. I had been close to Kaycee several times but was surprised to see that Kaycee looked like lots of other tiny ranch country towns. Just

Kaycee is a place where North Dakota means something other than "blizzard"

a little burg out on the prairie.

I knew I'd like Kaycee when the first thing I saw was the bucking horses in a little pasture on the edge of town.

I knew I'd like Kaycee when within 10 minutes I ran into a guy I'd met before. A fella with great stories about catching wild horses wherever wild horses are found in the west.

I knew I'd like Kaycee when the lady at the motel told me to save the cash I offered her and told me a personal check would be fine.

I knew I'd like Kaycee when I attended the free barbecue and rodeo slack Friday evening. Wasn't long before I had met a bunch of people, both Kaycee residents and people just there for the rodeo.

You can't help but enjoy a town where you can have breakfast at a place called the Feed Rack and drink coffee 'til the parade starts Saturday morning.

The bucking horses lead the parade. The rest of the parade is mostly kids, horses, or kids on horses. There are Shriners in the parade but they ride buckskins instead of motorcycles and there is no city ordinance against a few horse turds in Kaycee. As usual, the local fire department trucks are in the parade. As usual they blow their sirens, but these firemen turn their hoses on each other now and then, too.

There was only one milk cow in the parade, but if you carefully analyze the situation, one milk cow is enough in any parade.

There aren't too many entries in the parade, but in small town fashion, they space them out well. It was a great parade!

Kaycee is a place where North Dakota means something other than "blizzard"

The single steer roping was good. The horses really bucked. Bareback rider Larry Sandvick, formerly of Killdeer, now of Kaycee, made a spectacular ride and won third. I was surprised to see Dan and Don Miller of Raleigh, ND, entered in the bareback riding. They didn't place, but rode good enough to make you proud of them. The rodeo was first class.

An added bonus was a pile of used baling wire in perfect condition I found behind the chutes. I carefully gathered it and put it in my car. It is a good feeling knowing I can deduct the mileage to Kaycee as a "parts run." It was fun to go to a place where people seemed to be more proud of their neighbors than they were of themselves. A young fella points to an old cowboy, as slim as the last roll-your-own in a sack of Bull Durham. "That's Norris Graves, the toughest fella you ever saw. Had lip cancer once. Cut it off with a jack knife and then daubed dehorning paste on it so it wouldn't grow back." Later, I learned Norris won the bareback riding and won second in bronc riding at a Kaycee rodeo in 1932 at age 12. I heard lots of stories about many Kaycee cowboys, young and old.

It was great to go somewhere where the words "North Dakota" meant something other than a blizzard. It was "Oh, you're from North Dakota, huh? Do you ever see anything of Dean Armstrong? How's Delvin Reich doing? Brad is really riding good again this year. Tell Dale Jorgenson that Russ Taylor says hello," and so on. A bronc rider from Kaycee credits Duane Howard for much of his riding skill. I heard a great story about Alvin Nelson, Pete Fredericks, and Jim Tescher that I had never heard before. My face hurt from smiling.

Take a firm grip on a hoof rasp sometime. That's what a handshake feels like in Kaycee. It was a good feeling to have someone shake your hand and tell you that they hoped to see you again next year. It was a better feeling knowing that they meant it.

Good Lord willing and the crick don't rise, I'll be there!

Up Sims Creek

By: Rod Nelson

At least in the Fall people with ugly legs quit wearing shorts

Times are great here at Sims. Fall colors have arrived. Those folks who are really fond of brown are ecstatic. The hills are brown, the yard is brown, most everything is brown. Even my clothes are brown a good share of the time, although they usually get that way when I get too close to a cow.

Theoretically, fall is a great time of the year. Many people claim fall is their favorite. I like the fall quite a lot, too, although I am not exactly sure why. Perhaps it's because fall means the harvest. For ranchers that means it is soon time to sell calves. It used to be fun to sell calves when they brought enough money to repay the money borrowed against them.

We prairie dwellers have to admit that the fall color deal is a tad over-rated. It's OK if you happen to be there on that day when it happens, but not everyone is that lucky.

It is possible to go to church on a Sunday morning, have the preacher get carried away a bit on a long-winded sermon, and miss the fall color deal completely. Nothing left but a few scraggly, naked trees standing there. If that happens you have to be content with the secondary fall colors. Those are the piles of yellowish leaves drafted up here and there on the ground.

There are some occasions when one can enjoy more spectacular secondary colors or spectacular secondary horizontal colors. That's when the east wind is strong enough to send bunches of Minnesota leaves our way. Such viewing is nice, but requires the use of safety glasses.

I guess there are plenty of reasons to enjoy fall.

It gets cold enough in the fall to finally kill the flies and grasshoppers, but still leaves most people alive.

At least in the Fall people with ugly legs quit wearing shorts

It gets nicer to go shopping, as people with ugly legs quit wearing shorts. This alone does much to improve the scenery.

Fall is that gap in between the heat of August and mid-winter deep freeze. It is a nice time to dream of all the great and fun things you could be doing if you had your work caught up.

That's the bad thing about fall. There is never time in the fall to do fall things. There are always too many left-over summer things to do. I'm not sure what the "fall" things to do are, as we have traditionally ruined this time of year as catch up time or last-minute get-ready-for-winter time.

Fall often means pouring concrete and having to cover it so it won't freeze, or frantically hauling hay before a snowstorm or countless other last minute tasks.

Sometime, if I live long enough, there will be a great year. The weather is going to be so nice from early in the spring and all through the summer, and nothing will break down all through the season. I will be full of ambition and by September 15th I will have nothing to do but enjoy the fall.

Hate to be a pessimist, but I'll bet we have an early winter.

Up Sims Creek

By: Rod Nelson

Perfecting the art of hugging without touching

Times are tough here at Sims. The missus won't admit her age yet she claims I don't act mine.

I've been trying to reverse the aging process the last couple months. I try to run three miles most mornings. I was 47 years old in August and I'm already down to about 44.

It really feels good to get out there and run, especially since the pups go with me every day. They are really happy to see me in the morning. Each pup hopping up and down and fighting for position to get petted. Reuben, my Red Heeler, is just as happy to see me as the little pups.

It's funny how easy it is to show affection to animals, at least to those of us who really like animals, and it's just as easy to pet an old horse or dog as it is to pet a colt or puppy. People don't necessarily treat each other the same way.

In my case I am not sure if it was an ethnic trait or not, but much attention was given to little children. I know all of us in my family were shown plenty of affection and all of us continue to show lots of affection to little kids. As we grew older, however, I think it was expected that we get more reserved.

I don't remember much hugging and carrying on at my family reunions, although there were a couple aunts who would squeeze you till you fainted if they got a hold of you. More common were my relatives who had perfected the art of hugging without touching.

We just didn't seem to need much of that hands-on stuff. The first time I can remember touching my mother was when she shook my hand when I graduated from high school.

Times have changed since then. Now that my mother is 80 years old, it seems

Perfecting the art of hugging without touching

natural and easy to give her a hug and kiss. I still like my relatives best; however, one or two at a time, so we can enjoy a pleasant conversation over a cup of coffee.

The missus' family is quite a lot different than mine. The missus' idea of a good time is a hundred of her relatives in one room. Walk into one of their gatherings and you are in for some serious hugging. They remind me a lot of my pups.

I'll give them credit though because no matter how many of them are around, they find some way to show you some individual attention.

They had a big party last week for my father-in-law's birthday. I arrived with a fresh wound on my forehead. A couple days before, a big cow had kicked the center gate of my trailer back into my head as I tried to load her. It wasn't a bad wound in ranch country; only lost a couple quarts of blood.

I knew it wasn't pretty, but was surprised that a couple holes that weren't even festering would bother some people so much. A big fella at the party finally asked me if I would please put a Band-aid on it and I obliged.

We got into a pretty good visit for quite a while and I didn't pay much attention to the rest of the group until I heard gales of laughter in the next room.

I rounded the corner and there they were – thirty people and the family dog – all with a Band-aid on their forehead!

Up Sims Creek

By: Rod Nelson

Politicians should add pizzazz to negative advertising

I thought times were tough here at Sims, but I was talking to my friend Ted from Hannover the other day, and he said things were so bad at his place that his dog moved over to the neighbors. This dog liked to keep in touch, however, and always came home for birthdays and holidays.

Speaking of dogs, I hate to brag, but one of those composite pups I raised is so smart she is sending us letters from her new home in northern Minnesota.

I gave up waiting for a good snowstorm and hauled my hay home. It's not much of a challenge on bare ground, but it looks like the ground will be frozen solid soon and when it does freeze, I want to be able to get right at digging some post holes.

Hauling hay isn't a bad job. I have a cab on my tractor and can listen to the radio. I don't get to watch much television. The missus thinks there is too much smut on it for me. I was just starting to learn some things when she cut me off. Anyway, I really caught up a lot on the news listening to that radio.

One thing I noticed is that there sure have been a lot of political ads on the air. The candidates are really trying hard to get elected. I would imagine these people are out of work, can't get a real job, and really do need to get elected to something.

I was really startled by one ad I heard yesterday. Attorney General Heidi Heitkamp ran a plain old political ad that made no mention of her opponent. I would have thought she had more imagination than that. Certainly she could have come up with something negative like everyone else.

At one time I didn't like the negative campaigns, but I am getting more fond of negative political ads all the time. I just wish they used a little more imagination. The typical negative ad usually claims their opponent has, will, or wants to raise taxes. Give us a break! They all are going to raise our taxes anyway.

Politicians should add pizzazz to negative advertising

I think a good negative ad should contain a lot of personal information, stuff that the public would enjoy hearing about, perhaps something like this: "My opponent not only voted for the largest tax hike in history, he also, according to a reliable source, never changed his underwear throughout the whole last legislative session."

Another good idea would be to mention their opponent's breath or degrees of body odor.

Perhaps some mention of their opponent's physical appearance would go over well. "Before you even think about voting for John Doe, have you taken a serious look at that sucker's nose lately?" or "Did you realize my opponent wears a size 14 shoe and a size six cap?"

A political ad could contain a little praise along with the criticism. "Yes, I'll admit my opponent is brilliant on foreign affairs, but do you realize what a sorry job he does of combing his hair over that bald spot?"

A desperate politician, way behind in the polls, might say: "My opponent not only is soft on crime, but believe it or not, folks, he chases his cattle with a four-wheeler!"

Rather than hear the usual bashing about fiscal irresponsibility and so on, wouldn't it be nice to hear something like, "My opponent went to the Almont lutefisk supper and just ate meatballs and lefse, no lutefisk at all! Can you trust such a person?"

I hope some of those politicians will heed my advice. Maybe the ads in the next election will be a little more interesting.

Up Sims Creek

By: Rod Nelson

Mountain Time leaves plenty of time for reading

Times are tough here at Sims. My loan officer used to feel sorry for me. This year I even feel sorry for him.

I sure don't care much for this Mountain Time when the days get so short. Yes, I know that the daylight is the same no matter what time we use, but it's mean when it's almost dark when the kids get home from school at four o'clock. It gets so bad that I have to do some of my chores.

I guess what bothers me the most about Mountain Time is the long, dark evenings. Six hours or so of sitting around the house waiting for bedtime is a long time. Even if the missus would let me watch TV, there is only so much of that crap I can stand.

The first thing I hanker for when boredom strikes is food. A fella can put away a lot of grub on a long evening. It's nothing to put away a five-pound roast and a loaf of bread in a short time while waiting for supper on a long winter evening.

Probably, the next thing I do to combat long evenings is visit on the phone, but there is a limit to how much my neighbors can stand, too.

My long-time remedy for long evenings has always been reading.

One of my favorite things in my mom's house was the end of the living room which was solid book shelves, top to bottom. If boredom struck, no matter how many times you had picked over the books stored there, you could always find one you hadn't read or maybe find one that had been last read so long ago it was time to read it again.

All types of books were in that bookcase. Cheap old western paperbacks, old school textbooks, novels, poetry books, lots of books of non-fiction – especially of the old west and pioneer days, heavy books, light books and an especially cherished complete set of 1949 encyclopedias.

Mountain Time leaves plenty of time for reading

When I think of my Dad on a long winter evening, I would no doubt think of him sitting in his chair with a book in his hand. I guess some things are definitely inherited, as I see my children, especially my daughter, with books in their hands much of the time on long winter evenings as well.

We don't have a bookcase like Mom had, but thanks to my handyman father-in-law, we do have a modest bookcase crammed with a variety of books. We even have the same old set of 1949 encyclopedias.

I am proud of the books in our bookcase. They are nothing fancy and contain the same types of books that Mom's bookcase held, but there is a certain satisfaction just seeing them there. Stored in those shelves is a lot of entertainment as well as information.

Lots of people, knowing my love of reading, have given me books through the years. I also can't help browsing through used book stores and have bought some dandy books at auction sales.

I have probably acquired most of my books by borrowing them and not returning them. That is a good, cheap way to get a bunch of quality books without spending much.

I also cannot help but lend books to others. It is nice to have others enjoy the same books that were of special interest to us. I try, however, to lend only to those who will return them.

One of my favorite reference-type books is a book on horse training called Breaking and Training the Stockhorse by C.O. Williamson. I borrowed this book from a friend about 10 years ago. This book is so good I have no intention of ever returning it. I also will lend this book to no one.

I still cannot resist buying new books now and then. Once in a while you find something that cannot be passed up. Once in a while you find something that you realize is really special.

Mountain Time leaves plenty of time for reading

A couple such books were written by a friend of mine, Russell Gietzen of Glen Ullin, ND. These books, "A Dakota Boy Goes to War," and "A Dakota Boy at War," are a collection of letters Russell sent to family members during service in Vietnam.

I was amazed at these letters that Russell sent home. Russell has not doctored these letters. They are original and intact. Russell stresses that these letters were written by an 18-year-old farm boy who had never been more than a few miles from home, and only reflect his observations and views of that time in his life.

Russell's descriptions of army life, Vietnam, and the Vietnamese people through the naive eyes of a farm boy are fascinating. Some day, a hundred years from now, Russell's letters will be discovered and will go down in history as an incredibly honest account of a soldier's tour in Vietnam. Russell won't live long enough to cash in.

The first two books take the reader only about halfway through Russell's first tour. When Russell sells enough books he will no doubt come out with the next edition.

You can read 22nd century literature today merely by ordering Russell's books. At $12 plus $1.50 postage each, they are not cheap for paperback books, but I would highly recommend them to anyone who would like to make productive time out of a long winter evening.

Russell's address is 6780 County Road 140, Glen Ullin, ND 58631-9757.

Some friends of mine told me a couple weeks ago that for good humor it's hard to beat books written by Dan Cushman. Especially recommended was a book of his no longer in print called "Stay Away Joe." I have not been able to find this book. If anyone knows where I might find a copy let me know. I would like to borrow one.

That's it for the Critic's Corner.

Up Sims Creek

By: Rod Nelson

A kid could learn a lot from bachelor farmers/ranchers

Times are tough here at Sims. This is the first time I have ever had the Christmas spirit before Thanksgiving. It must be something to do with the weather.

It darn sure has been winter-like weather. More snow here than usual and the cows really have an appetite. I guess it must be worse south of Glen Ullin as Leonard told me the smoke has been freezing solid coming out of his stovepipe. He claims he has to go up on the roof now and then and cut the smoke off with an ax. Almost killed his neighbor when a large chunk of smoke hit the ground one day.

Had a nice bachelor Thanksgiving as the missus and kids were gone. Oh, I could have gone several places for dinner, but I just never got around to it. I don't know why the women talk about how much work it is to make Thanksgiving dinner. Didn't take me long, and sow belly and eggs are mighty tasty, too. I liked it so much I had the same thing the next morning for breakfast.

I guess women wouldn't appreciate a lot of bachelor meals. When I was a kid, I enjoyed a lot of meals with bachelors. Mostly old bachelors. Fried pork was pretty common with the bachelors around home. I guess fried beef was common, too. Fried potatoes were a favorite. Fried eggs were for sure. You might get fried venison sometimes depending on the time of year. Fried pancakes with fried sausage was always good and sometimes you may be treated to fried liver and onions. Dessert, if offered, was almost always ice cream.

The bachelor farmer/rancher is getting to be a rarity. That is a great loss for rural America. It was a great place for a kid to go. Bachelors always looked forward to company stopping in.

It seemed like the bachelors had the best stories to tell. Of course when your audience is a young boy who never had done much, I suppose the opportunity existed to embellish things a bit.

93

A kid could learn a lot from bachelor farmers/ranchers

A kid could learn a lot from these old bachelors. They seemed to be authorities on most everything from sex to politics to religion. They also could tell you most anything about ranching you might want to know. I suppose it is understandable that a bachelor would have such strong convictions. After all, a bachelor wouldn't have his views challenged nearly so much as a married man.

Another thing a kid could learn is that a little dirt won't kill you. Although some bachelors kept a neat and clean house, the average bachelor was casual as far as housekeeping goes. I ate lots of meals with my bachelor friends, but not everyone could enjoy a meal in such conditions.

I remember a birthday party at Olaf's place one time. The women went to the kitchen to fix some lunch. "Olaf," my mother said, "there are mouse tracks in your frying pan."

"Oh, they'll go away when you heat it up," Olaf said.

We made regular visits to the bachelors in our area. Martin was another favorite. He was a kind, friendly man with a perpetual twinkle in his eye. Always tickled when we stopped in, he would always insist we have a cup of coffee. He always cooked his coffee really slow. He could keep his guests a lot longer that way. His stories about his youth in Wisconsin or any of his other countless stories or jokes always made the wait worthwhile.

Charlie worked for two old maid ranchers who lived close to us. Born in 1880, he lived to be 106. Strangely enough, he never talked much about the real old days. A man who bought his first car at age 57 could have lots of stories, one would think, but he preferred to talk mostly about when I was a little boy and used to run away from home and go to "Charlie's" place. I remember Charlie giving me a fairly fresh empty Copenhagen box and I would march in the house, hand it to Emma and say

A kid could learn a lot from bachelor farmers/ranchers

"fill it up." Emma would go right to the cupboard and fill it with raisins for me. Charlie and I would each take a pinch and go to work. Anytime Mom would miss her five-year-old son she would check "Charlie's" place first.

I heard the same old stories from those old bachelors time after time. Lord knows how I would like to hear them one more time. All the old fellas from when I was a kid are gone. It would be quite a treat to hear MG tell me one more cowboy story, Olaf tell again about how bad the fights got at the dances, Martin tell a good joke; to hear one more time about when Charlie shot the big mule deer buck the week before season, or just to walk up on great-uncle Albert's porch one more time and hear him playing "Beyond the Sunset" on his piano.

I always appreciated the honesty of the bachelors, however tactless they may have been.

I remember bringing my new bride to see my friend Charlie. "Charlie," I said, "we got married." Charlie, who was 100 years old at the time, said, "Oh that's too bad, you could have been friends."

More recently, a bachelor cousin of mine complimented me on one of my last columns. "I really enjoyed that column about the books," he said. "It sure beats that mindless drivel you wrote about the week before."

Up Sims Creek

By: Rod Nelson

Rancher's Lament or "The cows they are a'munchin'"

This winter '97
is difficult I'd say,
You can tell it on the cowherd
by the way they're eating hay.

They're munchin' at a record pace,
Their appetite is vast.
At the rate the hay is going
the feed pile may not last.

Cows keep getting cheaper
but the cost of feed's a fright.
The outlook isn't rosy
with spring still out of sight.

It doesn't take a genius
to know ranchin' cannot pay
when hungry cows consume their worth
or more of it in hay.

But somewhere in the future
there's money to be made.
Cows will all be fat again
and bills will all be paid.

So we have to keep on working,
tho it will be no small feat,
to keep on raising cattle
'til they're worth more than they eat.

Up Sims Creek

By: Rod Nelson

You need good hobbies to make long winters enjoyable

Times are tough here at Sims. I am the only critter on the place that isn't getting thin. I'd hate to face this winter on a vegetarian diet. I can't remember ever spending more time outside and staying this warm. Anytime the missus needs to find me, she merely looks for a vapor trail. Anyone who suffers from the cold probably needs to include more meat and butter in their diet. I heard of a fella whose wife is on one of those low fat diets. I guess he has to turn the space heater on her just to get her out of bed in the morning.

This is quite a winter! A lot of people are in a world of hurt. I don't mean the inconvenience of having your driveway blocked, of missing some high school basketball games, paying extra for winter heat, or even dairy farmers having to dump milk now and then. There are too many stories of entire herds of cattle lost to worry about the minor problems of winter.

I have to confess that as a general rule I enjoy winter. I used to enjoy it more when I lived up on the Mouse River at Towner. The winter was a little colder there and the snow lasted a little longer. The best thing was that I had more cattle to feed and could stay outside longer. I remember a year ago it was merely a minus 38 degrees here at Sims and I heard on the radio it was 52 below up in Towner. I sure hated to miss that!

I have a hard time with people who complain about North Dakota winters. You would have to be crazy not to enjoy winter here in North Dakota. After all, winter is kind of our reward. As soon as the frost goes out of the ground, all our energy and resources are geared toward the next winter. Spring, summer and fall slip by before we can really enjoy them. Winter is the only season we have that really seems to last. Winter stays around long enough for us to really savor it.

I think the problem most people have is that they don't have enough good winter hobbies. I have always tried to find good hobbies that make winter more enjoyable.

You need good hobbies to make long winters enjoyable

One of my hobbies is encouraging the missus to shovel the sidewalk. Another hobby is encouraging the kids to shovel the sidewalk. A third hobby is shoveling the sidewalk.

I enjoy a lot of pickax work in the winter. Anytime you have livestock you can spend many happy hours picking out doors, gates, feed bunks, and horse stalls.

Thawing out water pipes and or water fountains is a favorite. It is hard to describe the pleasure of thrashing around on the ground with your head stuck in a water fountain, working barehanded on some frozen pipes, and watching your fingers turn white when it is 30 below. Even the cattle seem to enjoy watching you work. I envy mobile home owners who get that sort of recreation all the time.

Pushing snow on an open air Oliver with an F10 Farmhand rates high on my list of good winter fun. It is hard to measure the excitement level of piloting that old Farmhand at high rates of speed into rockhard drifts of snow. Also, many happy afternoons can be spent welding on that old Farmhand.

In a winter such as this one there are always tales of heroism and incredible stories of survival. One of my favorites this winter involved my old pard, Dean, who was snowbound for several days without snoose. He finally heard of a neighbor with a one-ton four-wheel-drive pickup who was going to try to get to town for supplies. Dean got a hold of this guy and asked if he could please bring him a box of snoose.

"No problem," the neighbor assured him. "We'll drop it off on the way home."

Dean was salivating heavily when the pickup bearing the snoose came into view. The pickup stopped on the highway and a young boy headed up to Dean's home with the precious box of Copenhagen. Dean, in wild excitement, met the young fella at the door. Somehow the young lad had lost the box on the way to the house and all search efforts failed to locate the missing snoose. No one will ever know how

You need good hobbies to make long winters enjoyable

the boy survived. The last I heard Dean was chewing on some old cigarettes while he waited for the snowplow.

Many years ago my friend, Dale, was in a similar situation. Snowbound for days without tobacco, he decided to ride three miles through the storm to an old bachelor's place. He knew the bachelor chewed snoose and figured the old boy would have some extra tobacco around the place. The old bachelor wasn't home. Dale admitted later that he ransacked the shack and found no snoose anywhere. "You know, I hated that old guy for several years after that storm!"

Up Sims Creek

By: Rod Nelson

Parents – bound and gagged – would enhance high school athletics

Times are pretty darn good here at Sims. It has been a pretty easy winter for me compared to the winter many in the area have had. It seems as if everyone would like to claim that the winter or snowfall has been especially tough in their own area. Most of us don't have to look far to find someone who has suffered more than we have.

I can't remember ever having better service with snow removal on our county roads. There were a few days when the roads were blocked around here, but it was storming so bad those days no one but a fool or a milk truck driver would attempt to be out there. An area dairy farmer told me that the fella who picks up his milk never missed a day. I don't see how he made it. A couple of those days I think the visibility was even less than zero.

At any rate I think milk truck driver is another occupation that I would like to avoid, along with county blade man. The county blade man has always had to endure the criticism of all the rural population. Everyone seems to feel that he is the blade man's boss. The blade man probably endures more unjust criticism than most public employees.

This winter I have added two more jobs to my list of things I would not care to do. Coach and referee.

As a high schooler, I played football. I am not sure why I played football. I suppose it was because the other kids played football and I wanted to be part of the crowd. At any rate I guess I thought I had a good time playing football. My folks, like many rural parents at the time, cared nothing about football or any other school sports. My folks, like many other parents, did not attend ball games, at least not very often. I can only remember seeing my dad at one game. I can remember seeing him standing on the sidelines, desperately looking for someone else who cared nothing for the game to visit with.

Parents – bound and gagged – would enhance high school athletics

I can't remember wishing that Dad cared about football. He neither criticized nor encouraged my involvement. He did care, however, about my academic progress in school. No high school coach or referee had any problem with my dad.

My kids are now old enough to participate in school athletics. They really appreciate it if their folks attend the games. They appreciate it so much that I attend all the games I can.

I probably have inherited too many of Dad's traits. I cannot be a really good booster. Cheering is not my bag. Perhaps the torture of sitting on the bleachers makes me unable or unwilling to get too much into the spirit of the game. I do find the games entertaining. It is fun to see my kids doing something they enjoy so much. I enjoy seeing them make a good play now and then. I enjoy watching the neighbor kids play. Like my dad, I enjoy the people around me. I enjoy the visiting. Like my dad, I have little respect for people who are a little too proud of their kids. Like my dad, coaches and referees come under little fire from me.

Perhaps I know too little about ball games. I can't tell traveling from a double dribble.

I can see a lot in a bronc ride. I can tell when a cowboy misses a horse out. I can tell whether or not he turns his toes out. I can see if he rides loose or if he is in trouble. I can tell if the horse is easy or hard to ride. I was never a good bronc rider, but I have been on quite a few broncs.

I have seen a lot of really bad rodeo judges. I have criticized a lot of rodeo judges. I never remember myself or any other cowboys hanging over the bronc chutes and verbally attacking a judge. Their decision, bad as it may be, was the decision of the day.

Like my dad, I think high school athletics would be enhanced if all the parents were bound and gagged at the games.

Up Sims Creek

By: Rod Nelson

This year's tax extension allows for ample reading time

Things are picking up here at Sims. Along with Lincoln's and Washington's birthday, February 15th will go down as an important date.

This is the day bare ground was sighted at Sims for the first time in the winter of 1997. Admittedly it was only on the top of a hill similar in height to the Matterhorn, but it was nice to see it anyway. The kids took turns looking through the binoculars at the phenomenon. They wanted to climb the hill and see it closer, but we didn't dare chance it in case of a storm. We told them if it warmed up by the middle of May we would try it then.

I have heard quite a few interesting comments about the winter. I heard one fella mention that they were measuring the snow from A to Z, and they were up to their S's in snow. One of the best stories came from south of Steele where a farmer claimed the snowbanks were so high in his yard that his mercury vapor yardlight didn't go off until 10 o'clock in the morning and came back on again at two in the afternoon.

One stroke of good luck we had this winter was the extension we farmers and ranchers got on our income tax deadline. Since this once-in-a-lifetime extension puts April 1st instead of March 1st as the deadline, it has given me several extra days to finish reading several new books that arrived. I would normally start frantically working on my record book.

The books, "Grass Beyond the Mountains," "Nothing Too Good For a Cowboy," and "The Rancher Takes a Wife," are true adventure stories of the author, Richard P. Hobson, Jr. Hobson and his partner were working cowboys in Wyoming in the early 1930s. They heard stories of unexplored wilderness areas of British Columbia where they thought they might be able to start a real frontier ranch. They started up there in 1934, and in 1935 pushed over a mountain range and discovered a vast area of prairie, meadows, bog, muskeg, timber wolves, bears and Indians who had never seen a white man before their arrival.

Their true stories of moving herds of cattle into unmapped country and the hardship and trials of starting a ranching business on a huge scale 200 miles from the nearest frontier town are really fascinating. Consider hauling hay mowers and rakes over mountain passes on pack horses, or a frantic winter cattle drive of over 100 miles with 300 cattle to reach winter feed supplies. The trail was broken by a herd of horses driven ahead who also pawed enough snow at night to uncover some grass for the cattle.

This was not done in balmy North Dakota weather. The temperatures reached an honest -60 degrees F on some of the nights during the drive. The coldest temperatures in that area have been known to hit a -74 degrees.

It seems unreal to me that a real frontier existed as recently as the 1930s. Once again I find myself born too late!

The books were written in the early 1950s, but have been recently reprinted. I heard about them from some Canadian friends, and was able to order them from a Snohomish, WA bookstore.

I have always been interested in books of this nature. I suppose partly because we find ourselves so close to the development of this part of our country. After all, most people my age or older can recall conversations with early immigrants and homesteaders who talked about parts of the Dakotas and Montana where there were no roads or fences at the time they came here.

A good source of stories about early North Dakota and Montana ranching are the "Fifty Years in the Saddle" books. I have Volume Three which, I believe, contains all material printed so far. It is filled with good pictures and stories about early area

This year's tax extension allows for ample reading time

pioneers and ranchers.

This book can be ordered from Manfred Signalness, HC03 Box 2613, Watford City, ND 58854 for $38.50 plus $3 postage. Considering the size and content of this valuable area history book, it is a bargain! The "Fifty Years in the Saddle" people have put tremendous effort into the development of these books. This book has a special place in my library.

I sure hope we get another tax deadline extension; I still have quite a lot of reading left!

Up Sims Creek

By: Rod Nelson

Modern technology – it came too soon or I came too late

Times are tough here at Sims. I didn't realize how bad until I saw my tax man last week. We were going over my depreciation schedule when he paused, scratched his head and finally said, "You know, this machinery of yours is going to start appreciating in value pretty soon."

A friend of mine once told me, "Rodney, you are like the Unibomber. You know, anti-technology."

I really didn't think that was a fair statement. In fact, there have been times when I have almost considered using nylon ladigos. I will admit when they invented a telephone cord long enough so that you could visit with your neighbor and pee off the porch at the same time, I felt they had gone far enough.

I occasionally take a big stab at the modern world. Take last year for instance, when we purchased a computer. Not just any old computer either. This is a state-of-the-art modern computer with lots of memory, power and speed. I figured this machine should make me lots of money.

And now this winter I borrowed a team of mules. These are big mules standing 16 hands and weighing about 1400 pounds at least. I am not really a "Mule Man." I prefer horses, but these big gentle Jennys would provide me with a little winter entertainment, I thought.

I actually used the mules almost daily through December and January and sporadically since then. It would be hard to put a dollar value on what the mules made or cost me, but I would say that in all the bad storms my cows were munching hay in a very well protected spot – a spot that I couldn't have gotten to without the mules. I believe if I hadn't gotten the cattle to that place I probably would have had either some death-loss in my cow herd or at least some of the cows

Modern technology – it came too soon or I came too late

would have suffered some injury due to the extreme cold. At any rate, I know the cattle are in better condition due to the mules. In addition, I had the satisfaction of standing out in the storm on that hayrack instead of sitting in a heated cab. Such activity insures your right to eat anything and everything that you wish to throughout the winter.

I found that the mules were very interesting animals. Like any animal they can aggravate you now and then, but you have to admire them for their good points as well. They soon learned the routine and caused less problems than they solved. When they got themselves in a jam they would wait until I helped them out of it. I would say this is one of the best points of the mules. In a situation where a horse would get scared and possibly hurt himself, the mule seems to understand that he has to be patient. On the bad side, the mules also seemed to resent doing things that were not on their regular schedule.

At any rate, the mules showed obvious intelligence and no doubt are capable of rational thought.

My new computer never thought of anything all winter.

Nope, it just sat there running, hour after hour, not caring a bit about anything.

That is not to say I didn't enjoy the computer. I hope to get lot of good out of it sometime. I hadn't typed for 30 years and now have gotten almost proficient at typing again. I really like typing on the computer, as it is so easy to correct mistakes. The spell check is wonderful for people like me. I no doubt will learn how to do more and more things with the computer as I work with it.

The problem is that the mules are a lot easier to work with. The computer makes me a lot madder than the mules. If the mules lay down and refuse to work I know

Modern technology – it came too soon or I came too late

what to do. When this darn computer seizes up, I have to find help to get it going again. It is aggravating to have to go ask your 14-year-old daughter how to operate the equipment. It is more aggravating when the 14-year-old tells you to stay away from the computer when she is not around to make sure I will not goof up the machine.

I am not against modern technology. I just wish I had been born soon enough so I wouldn't have to mess with the stuff.

Up Sims Creek

By: Rod Nelson

Springtime on the ranch offers variety of activities

Times are still tough here at Sims, but at least winter is coming to an end. I have noticed a couple sure signs of spring lately. The geese have been flying north, the driveway looks like a canal and there are hardly any boxelder bugs left in the house.

This is a time of the year when I really feel fortunate. In fact, I think ranchers should celebrate Thanksgiving at this time of year. Stockmen are the only rural group that really have good spring activities or things to do.

Face it, summer means all types of activities for most all people, fall offers a variety of activities from hunting to photographing fall colors and winter is filled with good wholesome winter sports. But what does spring offer to many people? I must be a pretty mundane time for city people and rural dwellers who raise no livestock.

Spring, however, for the livestock producer means a variety of activity.

Animal lovers really love springtime on the ranch and the nice thing about spring is that you don't have to go outside to enjoy the livestock. Depending on the weather, you may find newborn calves anywhere from the entry to the bathtub. You know it is spring when the missus' hairdryer is always plugged in and lying on the floor in the entryway.

For many people spring is a great time for riding. It is always a pleasure to sit up high on a horse and check cattle. The really nice thing about it is that you are not restricted to just riding in daylight hours. There are many occasions when you can ride throughout the night, depending on the weather. The worse the weather, the more you get to ride.

Riding double is another fun thing. The only difference is in the spring the warm cuddly thing you have in your arms is not your girlfriend – it's a newborn calf you have to haul somewhere. It's been a long time since I had a girlfriend riding in front.

Springtime on the ranch offers variety of activities

I have noticed the newborn calves seem to fight a lot less.

For people who hate horses but raise cattle, spring means happy hiking. Not boring old hiking down a trail, but a challenging hike around the corrals. Going eye-to-eye with a protective new mother cow, or simply crossing certain boggy areas on foot and making it safely are times of great exhilaration.

Springtime is also a time of the year when ranchers feel inspired to buy things that they have put off for a long time. There is nothing like a new pair of overshoes to cheer one up. What could match the comfort of dry feet? That old ragged pair that made it through the winter just seem to lose their appeal in the spring.

Springtime is also a time when the rancher acquires a real unique identity. He gets a certain "air" about him. I think it has to do with wearing sodden clothes and wet gloves. No amount of washing can completely remove the odor. Hog producers and dairymen are always standouts in a crowd, but the rancher's fragrance is strongest in spring.

It's a funny feeling to get all cleaned up, dressed in your best to go to church and sit there a while, when all at once you realize you live in a rural area by that unmistakable rancher aroma that comes drifting toward you. It's a funnier feeling when you realize it's coming from your missus!

Up Sims Creek

By: Rod Nelson

Life in the monastery seems to suit this cowboy just fine

After watching the news about Grand Forks, things look pretty good here at Sims. I thought I lost a lot in the early April blizzard.

I guess us baby boomers finally have "our winter." I mean the one we can always refer to. It's going to be hard to top it for a long time.

I was visiting with a young couple from the Beulah-Knife River area the other day. Jack and Mardee Reich got married in May last year. Mardee is from Kansas and in her first year in North Dakota she has been through "the 100-year winter," "the 100-year blizzard," and "the 100-year flood."

For livestock producers, the April blizzard really put a finishing touch on a devastating winter. I will never forget this blizzard as it will go down in my history as the time I joined the monastery.

Just a few days before the storm I was watching a late night TV show. Dana Carvey was a guest on the show and he mentioned he was raised a Lutheran, which he said was kind of like being "Catholic Light." I chuckled over that comment for several days, never dreaming I would have a real "Catholic" experience so soon.

The storm hit Friday night when I was in Dickinson. It was impossible to drive that night so I thought I would wait for morning, hoping things might be a little better. Saturday morning's road report only said "travel not advised," which we North Dakotans hear all the time. With stock at home to care for, I knew I had to take the chance.

As soon as I got out of town I knew I shouldn't be out there. The road was heavy with snow and visibility was next to nothing. About 16 miles out of town I finally came to a stop, hopelessly stuck. I thought of a book about angels we have lying around the house. I said to myself, "I could sure use one of those angels about now."

Life in the monastery seems to suit this cowboy just fine

In about a minute a big Kenworth pulled up alongside and the driver offered me a lift.

I don't know if he was an angel or not, but I am going to check and see if there really is a trucker from Kellogg, ID by the name of Walt Morris.

Walt didn't seem to need to see the road to drive. I couldn't see anything, but Walt made steady progress until we came upon a Greyhound bus stuck under an overpass east of Richardton. The Highway Patrol was there and had arranged for a snowplow to pull the bus out, and then the bus, a few trucks and other vehicles got turned around and we went back to Richardton in a little convoy.

With no power in the town, by evening the only logical place to go was the Richardton Abbey.

It was an eerie feeling at first. It seemed like entering an old castle. Monks in long robes leading us around the dark passages of the old building. If the monks had candles instead of dim flashlights and there had been lightning and thunder instead of a raging blizzard outside, I would have thought I was in Transylvania for sure.

It didn't take very long before I had a really good attitude about the monks. Within a couple of hours, several seemed like old friends. They couldn't have been nicer or more accommodating. They fed us right away, gave us blankets and a spot on the floor.

I wouldn't say that sleep was heavenly, but it sure beat the great outdoors.

Monks eat pretty early in the morning. I was glad they did. There was a lot to see at the Abbey. After church, several of the monks gave us tours. Brother Victor, a kindly elderly fellow who has lived most of his life there, showed us a small but very interesting museum. Afterward, he answered questions about the Abbey and the life of a monk. He chuckled a little when he told about a group of children that had

Life in the monastery seems to suit this cowboy just fine

once taken the tour with him. When he asked if there were any questions, a little girl raised her hand and asked if monks wore pants under their dresses. That pretty well took care of my next question.

By the time the noon meal was finished, I was ready to do something to help get my mind off my cattle, only 50 miles away. The Abbey has a sizable cowherd and I asked Brother Placid, the main herdsman, if I could be of any help. He seemed very appreciative that I offered, and we worked hard all afternoon pulling calves, getting cows and calves paired up, feeding hay, shoveling snow and other chores. We had to hustle to get back up to the Abbey for evening prayers.

With something like 40 monks around the place, I mentioned to Brother Placid that it must be nice to have such a labor force to dip into. Brother Placid paused a little, and said, "Well, not really. This type of life tends to attract mostly intellectuals."

It was at that point, I mentioned to Brother Placid that I would be interested in joining the monastery, but what could I do with the missus and the kids?

"Well," Brother Placid said. "Your wife could enter a convent and you could send your kids to an orphanage."

"Sounds okay so far," I said. "What sort of duties do you think I would get here?"

"We'd no doubt have you working with the cowherd," Brother Placid smiled.

It was then that I figured I might as well go back to Sims.

Up Sims Creek

By: Rod Nelson

Planning nephew's summer stay at the Nelson Ranch

Things are picking up here at Sims. A dry spot showed up on the driveway last week. It was great. We all took turns standing on it.

The missus' brother and his family live in Billings. We don't get together very often but do enjoy an occasional visit, usually when they are back in North Dakota. During a visit last fall someone suggested that we may like to have their son, Nathan, come out to Sims and spend the summer with us. I was a bit apprehensive at first. Just how could we entertain a kid from the big city and keep him happy all summer? I finally realized if his visit was to be successful, I would have to do a little planning. I decided to work up a summer work schedule so Nathan could be prepared for the summer activities. I felt this would clear up any questions ahead of time and help Nathan really prepare for his summer with his Uncle Rod.

I sent this schedule to Nathan and his folks:

* 5 a.m.: Uncle Rod and Nathan go for a three-mile run. Nathan should have some knowledge of CPR in case Uncle Rod should tip over. This is usually a pleasant run followed by some calisthenics.

* 5:45-6 a.m.: Time set aside for Nathan's personal hygiene.

* 6-6:40 a.m.: Nathan gives Uncle Rod a good Swedish-style massage.

* 6:40-7:15 a.m.: Breakfast. (This is a great time of day as Uncle Rod, with just a little prompting, will relate tales of the old days, especially of the early '60s when teenagers had to work a lot harder than teens of today.)

* 7:15-8:30 a.m.: Tree hoeing. Not any sissy hoeing on the Nelson Ranch. This will be sweat-'til-your-underwear-is-soaked hoeing (great for physical fitness and good mental health). Nathan won't be alone out there – Uncle Rod will be riding around checking on his progress.

Planning nephew's summer stay at the Nelson Ranch

* 8:30 a.m.-Noon: Work of the day. There will be some field work, like haying and such. When there is no field work to do, we will find light work for Nathan like fencing or general repairs.

* Noon-12:20 p.m.: Free time. (Uncle Rod thinks all work and no play would make Nathan a dull boy.)

* 12:20-6 p.m.: Back to "Work of the day."

* 6-6:30 p.m.: Nathan will top off any new broncs on the Nelson Ranch.

* 6:30-6:40 p.m.: Nathan gets time off for personal hygiene.

* 6:40-7 p.m.: Nathan tops off more broncs.

* 7-7:40 p.m.: Uncle Rod will teach Nathan the fundamentals of steer wrestling. (Nathan will get to jump as many steers as he wishes off Uncle Rod's colts.)

* 7:40-7:50 p.m.: Nathan gets time off for personal hygiene.

* 7:50 p.m.-dark: Nathan will run the roping chutes while Uncle Rod and friend practice team roping and will care for horses when Uncle Rod heads for house.

* 10:15-10:30 p.m.: Suppertime.

* 10:30-11 p.m.: Nathan massages Uncle Rod's feet and clips toenails when necessary. (This will be another great bonding time as Uncle Rod can relate more tales of the old days.)

* 11:15-11:25 p.m.: More free time for Nathan.

* 11:25 p.m.: Bedtime. Nathan gives his aunt and uncle a big hug and hits the hay.

Planning nephew's summer stay at the Nelson Ranch

I believe the key to giving a city kid a good healthy experience out on the ranch or farm is good communication. I think this schedule was a good step in insuring his stay here at Sims would be a good one.

Unfortunately, the last time I talked to Nathan, it sounded like he had some new summer duties in Billings that would make his visit to Sims impossible this year.

Rats! I was really starting to look forward to Nathan's visit.

Up Sims Creek

By: Rod Nelson

Spring tests your fencing skills (and those of your neighbors)

Things are picking up here at Sims. Spring is on the way. With any luck the snowbanks should be melted by the first of June.

I have pretty much quit predicting an early spring for '97. I really felt with the early winter, spring would come early as well. Guess I was wrong.

Once in a while spring comes in textbook fashion. Late March brings early warm weather, the birds return from the south, crocuses bloom, calves are born on nice sunny days, and the whole prairie comes alive once more.

We need more textbook springs. If spring comes late, is interrupted often by late winter storms and calves are sick and unthrifty, spring holds little romance. The joyous part of spring doesn't come until it is almost over. Hopefully there is just a little time in between overshoes and summer heat.

One of the nice things about spring is that it gives us a chance to renew the skills we have learned through the years. Ranchers are fortunate to learn skills that few others could ever hope to learn.

Wire splicing is one skill that is really used a lot this time of year, especially if you happen to have hilly land. A novice can soon learn how to splice new wire, but it takes considerable skill to properly splice some of the wire that has been around for 80 years or so. This technique can soon be learned if you have long stretches of fenceline where the wires are broken between each post. Anyone who had lots of 20 and 30-foot snowdrifts on top of their fences soon learns proper splicing.

In really bad stretches of snow damage, you can spend as much time lifting steel posts up as driving posts down.

Fencing is really quite fun and relaxing. It is really a good way to pass the time. I enjoy it more and more, especially as my kids get older. It makes me feel like a

117

Spring tests your fencing skills (and those of your neighbors)

surgeon when I extend a hand and have one of my assistants give me the tools I need. It sure beats being out there alone. I think it will get even better in the future when I have my crew so well-trained that I can supervise from the pickup.

The best way to get your fencing done is to have a good pasture rotation system. Then all you need for tools is a good pair of binoculars. It is essential to know when your neighbor has just about gotten the job done. That is when you drive up and say, "Darn, you beat me to it."

Your most ambitious neighbors should have enough fence fixed so that you can safely turn out somewhere. Gradually, your other neighbors will eventually fix a little more. You may have to finally turn out livestock where the fence is truly poor. This still isn't a problem unless your grass is better than your neighbors! Sometimes I sure wish I had more pastures.

Up Sims Creek

By: Rod Nelson

Brandings are one of the last rural social events

Times are tough here at Sims. It's the time of year when the pessimists really come out of their cocoons. We just finished one of the worst winters in history and all they can talk about is drought and grasshoppers. I refuse to worry about either for at least a little while.

Doom and gloom provides a lot of entertainment for a lot of people, but I have to escape from that now and then, especially this time of year. The best cure for all that depression in May and June is to slip away to a few civilized brandings.

Civilized brandings are not to be confused with the solemn affairs where grim-faced people work calves slowly and painfully through some mechanical devise. The only entertainment is listening to the crack of a calf's hoof smacking the shins of the poor sap in charge of pushing the hapless critter into the chute. Perhaps a sadist may enjoy the grunts, groans and curses of some crew member smashing their fingers on some piece of iron.

Calf tables are basically antisocial devises. They were basically invented to eliminate the need for your neighbors. A small crew can work calves in these devises. If you don't need your neighbors to work calves, you probably won't have to help your neighbor either.

At a civilized branding, ropers heel the calves on horseback and drag them to the wrestlers who hold them briefly until the necessary tasks are done. I have never been to a civilized branding when it wasn't some kind of festive event. People come knowing it will be a good time.

There is usually a job for everyone who wants one. Hopefully enough young people, boys or girls, show up to do the wrestling. I have seen lots of 13-year-old girls who can hold the biggest calves. It is a real pleasure to watch good wrestling teams who

Brandings are one of the last rural social events

are well-experienced handle the biggest calves with ease as the horses bring them in. There is usually some entertainment value in watching big, athletic, but inexperienced, boys getting totally flattened by ordinary calves.

Lots of branding crews have an older hand who takes care of the branding fire and branding irons. There is even a job for someone who probably can only watch a gate. Children too little to wrestle calves probably will have some job like applying pine tar or carrying the oyster bucket.

Any heeler in a roping slump is bound to get some good-natured ribbing from someone. In fact, no one on a good crew is immune from some type of verbal abuse from their friends.

It doesn't take too much of a crew to work from 80-100 calves an hour. When the calves are turned out and the brawling stops, the best part of the branding is yet to come. A branding is one of the last rural social events where the cook goes all out to make a really memorable meal. You just can't beat the good food.

At a branding I was at last week I ate some of the best rhubarb pie and rhubarb dessert you can find. My hosts appreciated the compliments I made on these rhubarb treats. In fact, they even mentioned that the rhubarb came from a friend's garden. They went into some detail about how Joe took such good care of his rhubarb and watered it all the time. They seemed delighted to inform me that he would be coming over soon and I would get to meet him. When Joe did show up, they could hardly wait to introduce him to me.

You see, Joe was a German Shepherd-Husky cross.

I'll hand it to Joe. He knows how to make good rhubarb.

Up Sims Creek

By: Rod Nelson

Buying vs. producing milk – the very reason we honor dairy farmers

I've been seeing quite a bit of publicity about the dairy industry lately at June is Dairy Month. I don't know why they need June for Dairy Month as the dairy farmers get to milk those cows all year long.

As a tribute to the dairy farmers, I am going on record by saying that dairy products are a good bargain. I really couldn't tell you what a gallon of milk costs or the price of a pound of butter, but I know that going to the store is a lot better deal than producing it yourself.

I must have done a little grocery shopping back in 1985, as I decided we were spending way too much on dairy products. The simple solution would be to buy a nice milk cow. This friendly beast would provide us with all the fresh milk and butter we would need and still have enough left to feed her calf. My two little children would not lack for all the healthy milk they could drink and the visions of the missus churning butter were charming, to say the least.

I was in the front row at the March dairy sale in Mandan. Being a selective buyer and a former FFA dairy judge, most of the cows for sale that day didn't meet my specs. At last, the cow of my dreams stepped in the ring.

She was a 4-year-old Brown Swiss; long, tall, doe-eyed, heavy with calf and had a really nice set of long teats, perfect for milking.

The whole family had to go right up to the barn the next morning to see the new cow. Seems like everyone was impressed, especially my 3-year-old daughter. "Daddy, why does the cow need four brands?" she asked.

"Well, obviously this cow was loved by several people," I replied.

Wasn't long till the cow presented us with a nice calf. She was as good a mother as any range cow and I didn't even try to milk her for a week or so.

Buying vs. producing milk – the very reason we honor dairy farmers

The big day finally arrived and I headed up to the barn with a clean pail and high spirits.

I poured a generous portion of rolled feed in a tub, put it in a corner of the pen, roped her and gently tied her up. I grabbed a pail to sit on and sat up to milk the cow as she happily munched her grain.

It felt like a bomb went off on my chest. I don't know when I have ever been kicked harder. "Wow," I thought, "I must have startled her." I carefully sat down again and gently grabbed the handles. She didn't even stop chewing when she delivered a second, more powerful blow.

I'll admit I was slightly losing my patience by this time. As soon as I was able to breathe, I got another rope, put a Scotch hobble on her, and drew her left hind leg right up to her jaw. "Now kick, you old bag," I told her as I settled in for the third time.

She stood there real nice on three legs, but try as I might, I could not extract one drop of milk from her. I have never seen a critter that could hold her milk so well.

In desperation, I got her calf and let him suck. I had him penned separate since the night before and he was soon happily wringing his tail and having breakfast. When I could see that the milk was flowing freely, I pushed the calf aside and milked furiously while the calf sucked my left ear. She was an easy milker and it didn't take long till I had plenty for the house.

I proudly showed the missus the product of my labor and told her to rig up some kind of a strainer. A city girl, she asked why we needed to strain it.

"You'll find out," I told her.

I let the milk stand overnight in the refrigerator hoping to skim nice fresh cream the next morning for my breakfast.

Buying vs. producing milk – the very reason we honor dairy farmers

I believe gasoline would have a higher butterfat content than the milk from that cow. You could barely see any cream floating on the top the next morning. Undeterred, I thought at the least we had nice lowfat milk for the kids to drink. My 2-year-old son drank it pretty well, but my 3-year-old daughter didn't care much for it. She didn't seem to like our homemade milk and would only drink it under heavy pressure from her dad.

Every time we needed milk for the next few weeks, I went through the same routine. The snubbing post got shiny, the cow got really used to standing on three legs and many people commented on my "dishpan" ears.

I remember well when the wild onions came out. The milk smelled so strong the cats walked out of the barn. You couldn't feed the stuff to my daughter with a funnel. My son took a swig from his glass, wiped his mouth with the back of his hand and said, "Boy, I sure wish we could buy some milk." We have been buying it ever since!

The cow became a full-time range cow. She was like an old girlfriend who had split up with you on bad terms. She no longer looked pretty and always gave me a contemptuous, "I got the best of you" look every time she saw me.

She was around several years before she came up open in the fall. It was a festive occasion when I hauled her back to the sales ring.

Up Sims Creek

By: Rod Nelson

Around here, 4th of July and rodeos go hand-in-hand

Times are tough here at Sims. Like always, the Fourth of July comes around too darn soon. Dad always said the summer is over after the Fourth. I guess there is some truth in that statement as most rural people are so busy after that date, the rest of the summer blends into a blur. I guess that is why it is so important to celebrate the Fourth of July.

Many people celebrate the Fourth in strange fashions. Lots of people go to lakes, many go on picnics at parks or celebrate in other leisurely ways. They seem to think the Fourth of July should be cool, balmy, and pleasant. Not me, I only celebrate the Fourth in truly American fashion. I like it hot with clouds of choking dust. I have spent at least 35 July Fourths at rodeos.

As a kid, growing up in Towner, the Fourth of July rodeo was not only fun, but it was profitable as well. There was an exhibition chute on the corner of the arena and the area kids could ride all the calves they wanted at 50 cents apiece. I mean, they paid us to get on them. There was no shortage of pop or fireworks with a payday like that!

A few years later, I graduated to bucking horses. This seemed like a better deal, as now you could spend all the wages you earned elsewhere on entry fees in the hopes of winning a few dollars. The better you thought you were getting, the more rodeos you entered on the Fourth. This took away somewhat from the steady diet of Fourth of July dust, but replaced it with hours and hours of pleasant fellowship with four or five other guys crammed with your gearbags in some stifling hot car hurtling down the road at 80 miles an hour.

One of my most memorable July Fourths was 1978. I suppose I was at the Mandan rodeo on the 3rd and we were discussing how to make the run up to Towner and back to Raleigh and Mandan the next day. I was working on a construction job at the time and had spent some of my wages on a luxury 1972 Mercury Marquis. This

Around here, 4th of July and rodeos go hand-in-hand

machine had genuine air conditioning and only 99,000 miles on it. When I offered to drive, about five Bowman area cowboys dove into it like a pack of blue heelers and we were off. Most of those guys had never seen air conditioning before, much less a car with such low mileage.

We breezed up to Towner in fine shape. I noticed several of my old school teachers wiping their eyes with emotion as they saw me in my new car. They never thought I would be successful to that degree.

I recall nothing about the rodeo except that we got our horses as soon as possible and hurried back to the Mercury. We didn't have much time to make it to Raleigh. I gave the big Mercury her head as we rolled out on Highway 2. The boys were impressed with her speed as I kicked her down to pass a big semi. All of a sudden the big Merc shuddered violently. Someone said, "We blew a tire!" but I knew it was worse than that. Oil was all over the highway and there was a hole in the bottom of the oilpan. "Roll her in the ditch boys," I told my passengers. "I'll hitch a ride back to Towner and borrow a car."

It didn't take long to come back with a borrowed vehicle. All of my passengers except Cary Hande from Rhame had hitched a ride with someone else. Cary was sitting on his saddle on the side of the road looking sad and forlorn. He was too nice a guy to leave me, but I could tell he felt he'd never make it to Raleigh on time. "Don't worry, Cary," I told him. "I know all the back roads."

Cary mostly sat in silence on the trip. His only sign of emotion was the white in his knuckles as he gripped the seat tightly each time the borrowed Plymouth bottomed out on the gravel roads. Cary said later that the only time he saw pavement on the trip was when we crossed I-94.

Cary and I were sitting behind the chutes at Raleigh cleaning our fingernails when the weakhearts who abandoned us came puffing up with their gearbags.

Up Sims Creek

By: Rod Nelson

Summer means reunion time in rural North Dakota

Times are picking up here at Sims. We finally got under a couple thunderstorms in the last two weeks. The rain came just in time to save our grasshoppers.

Summer means reunion time in rural North Dakota. I recently went back to Towner for my 30th high school reunion.

Most small town high schools opt for all school reunions every few years. This is the best choice usually, but my class was bigger than average (44). We had a 20th class reunion and the majority felt we should have a 30th.

It seems to be hard to get people together for such an occasion. For those whose families have left the small rural towns, it would be hard to come back merely for a class reunion, but most of us still have the family members in the area which helps to justify the trip.

Living only 170 miles from Towner, it would have been a bit arrogant for me not to attend, when many came from considerable distances across the country. There was enough response from old classmates to indicate there would be fair attendance. Even some of them still living in Towner promised to come!

A wise man once told me that if you plan to attend a class reunion you should come looking either rich or slim.

I started my exercise program in earnest three months ago.

In the first couple months about all I accomplished was making my knees glow in the dark. I realized if I were to lose any weight I would have to do the unthinkable: "Eat less."

Eating less is a tough thing. You can quit tobacco. You can quit drugs or gambling, but you can't quit eating.

Summer means reunion time in rural North Dakota

The last 30 days I exercised every day and only ate enough for two men. I knew I was making progress when I was finally able to button my pants without lying on the bed!

A couple of days before the reunion I had my barber cut down the gray hair on my temples right down to the hide and told him to make the top look thick.

When the big day arrived I got up early, jogged all over the greater Sims area, had a cup of thin tea for breakfast, loaded the family and headed north. In a last ditch effort to shrink just a little more, I rolled the windows up tight and didn't use any AC.

It was a peaceful, quiet trip. The only sounds were the car humming and the labored breathing of my kids as they pressed their noses to the cracks around the windows hoping to get a little oxygen.

I was still a little nervous when I got to Towner and didn't go over to the reunion till later in the evening.

I was stunned when I walked in the place. Some of my old classmates had aged so badly they had a hard time recognizing me without hair.

It was a typical reunion. Lots of talk about the good old high school days. I can recall almost nothing about those years myself, so it was fun to hear about it.

I was glad I had come. It really was fun to see old friends and they had lots of good things to eat. I tore into the meal with the manners of a Blue Heeler. I ate like a coyote at calving season. It was great.

Anytime anyone aimed a camera, I squeezed in between a couple of fat guys. It is the easiest way known to look slim.

The reunion was over way too soon. It was all worth it when I heard someone say, "Rod sure looks good for as much as he eats!"

Up Sims Creek

By: Rod Nelson

Motion sickness is funny – unless you're the one suffering

Things are improving here at Sims. There are times when I can get both my kids working and I can find time to do something all by myself.

It still seems strange in some ways to be a parent. Many of my high school classmates are already grandparents while my children are only in their early teens.

I wonder sometimes if those of us who got started parenting later expect more from our children or do we just hope to see more of ourselves reflected in our children.

I was thinking of my two children the other day and I got to wondering about how many of their traits were inherited from me.

Several positive traits came to mind, but I realized I could not in good conscience take any credit for them. It came as a bit of a jolt that the one sure sign of their relationship to me was their susceptibility to motion sickness.

I hated any type of car travel when I was a kid; and my kids, especially my son, hate it as well.

I think part of my early hatred for traveling can be traced to my Dad's preference of cars.

Dad had one of the first VW Bugs. He loved those cars. Dad was a big man and he loved the head and leg room of the VW Bug. With the bucket seat jammed as far back as it would go, Dad could wear his hat in comfort in the VW.

Travel meant Mom and Dad and little sister up front, and me stuffed in between an older brother and sister in the windowless, airless back seat.

The elbowing, punching and squashing in the back seat were bad enough, but it was pure torture not to be able to see over the front seats or out the side windows. The situation always got worse when Dad fired up his pipe.

It wasn't long till my sister would yell, "Rodney is turning green again!"

Motion sickness is funny – unless you're the one suffering

When Dad got this warning, the VW would lurch to a stop by the side of the road, the doors would fly open and someone would grab me by the collar and drag me out in the ditch.

The scene is much the same today. Seems like we stop at most of the rest areas. I kind of enjoy it as I often visit with people from around the world as they exercise their pets and my kids throw up.

My older brother and sister still love to tell of how I used to turn green. Just a couple weeks ago, my sister laughed till she wiped away tears recalling my bouts of car sickness. I suppose it is funny. It is at least as funny as the flu or as entertaining as food poisoning. Everyone but the victim enjoys it alot.

Just a couple years ago I was in a six-passenger plane heading to Nevada. It was a nice flight till we went through some awfully turbulent air descending into Cody, WY to refuel.

It was bad enough going down, but the turbulence was even worse when we flew up through it again.

My discomfort was evident to my fellow passengers and they were enjoying it to the limit. My nephew (yes, big sister's son) really gave me a ribbing. "Hey, Uncle Rod, how are you doing? Feeling a little queasy? Ha! Ha! Ha!"

I finally had to ask for the little brown bag and I used it with relish. All of my tormentors in the close quarters of the plane soon found things to look at out the side windows. It was great to suddenly be the only one in the plane who now felt good!

Up Sims Creek

By: Rod Nelson

"He only cost a year's supply of snoose . . . ."

Like iron to a magnet
it happens without fail
Folks congregate or gather
when there's horses at a sale.

"Oh, I'm just here to watch, not buy,"
I heard a fella say,
"The missus claims she'd shoot me
if I bought a colt today!"

She asked, "Why'd you bring the trailer?"
Well, knowing what she thought
He told her that he brought it
in case the neighbors got one bought.

But, they mosey through the weanlings
like there's purpose to their trip –
"Gosh, that buckskin is a dandy,
and don't you like that bay colt's hip?"

"Ah, I'm not here to buy these horses,
Shucks, I've a couple I should sell,
But if I was really looking
Ain't that bald-faced bay colt swell?"

"He's not as big as several others,
but I don't like him any less,
His mother's just a young mare,
and milked real poor, I guess."

"You know, he just may be a sleeper,
I may bid once, just for fun –
He has the makings of a dandy,
and by gosh – he's bred to run."

When half the sale is over,
He says, "I haven't seen a dud,
They sure are selling good this year –
too rich for a poor man's blood."

"Aren't they some set of weanlings . . .
they're the best they've raised, I'll bet –
I'm not paying much attention . . .
have they sold that bay colt yet?"

"Now I'm not here to buy him –
I just like him awful well . . .
My hands are in my pockets,
But I'd like to see him sell."

"Just a few left in the sale –
it kinda strikes me strange,
The ones it seems I like the most
are priced out of my range."

"Heck, it's never smart to buy a colt,
they're overpriced, I'd say . . .
A four-year-old is always cheaper –
Hey wait! Here comes that bay!"

"He only cost a year's supply of snoose . . . ."

"Well, I really didn't need him,
but there's no way I could keep
my hands down in my pockets
when he was selling so darn cheap."

"You say the missus just passed out?
Oh, I think she'll be O.K. –
Here comes lot thirty-six,
that big stout, well-bred gray."

It's mighty quiet in the truck,
as they drive back to their place –
The missus' breath is coming heavy
disbelief shows on her face.

"Come on, Ma, lighten up,
you claim there's no excuse . . .
But heck, that bay colt only cost
a year's supply of snoose!"

"And I'm quitting, Ma, I promise,
When I finish this here can . . .
I had to buy that second one
when I saw the way he ran."

"These colts here have a future,
they are dandy ones, I'd say –
I can see them now as 2-year-olds –
They'll get better every day."

"You say we can't afford them,
Well, we're not sitting all that bad,
The market has been pretty good,
and it's the best calf crop we've had."

"You like him, Ma, now don't you?
He's by a son of Dash for Cash –
I think I'll let you name him . . ."
She mutters, "Too Much Cash!"

"Call the PCA tomorrow,
just say we have some bills –
They never seem to understand
why we use horses in our hills."

A horse is just a waste,
is the way those people think –
but dealing on an ATV
wouldn't make them blink!

They may have their facts and figures,
But it's plain to me, of course,
It's a sorry ranch that can't support
an extra saddle horse!

Up Sims Creek

By: Rod Nelson

Local celebration brings back memories of the old days

Well, I guess that summer is over. The school buses are running again.

Years ago summer wasn't over till after Labor Day. Labor Day was probably the most important holiday for us kids after Christmas and Easter. Labor Day was the day of the B and U Riders annual rodeo at the Herb Natwick arena at Bantry.

The Bantry rodeo was probably more of a neighborhood social than a rodeo. There was bareback and bronc riding and calf roping, but there were lots of events for kids and casual riders. Things like sack races, musical chairs, matched pair contests and cow and calf riding.

We usually started practicing for the Bantry rodeo as soon as the frost went out of the ground. A whole lot of calves and cows were bucked out at Dad's place all summer long in hopes of winning a ribbon in the calf riding or a check in the cow riding.

I still have my third prize ribbon for calf riding in 1956. I guess it was the highlight of my rodeo career. It went down steady after that.

Even if you didn't plan on entering any rough events, a kid sure enough wanted at least to ride in the grand entry. It didn't matter if you didn't have a fancy outfit. Lots of kids rode bareback on pretty plain horses and probably even had to wear clodhoppers or farmer shoes. There was still something special about riding in that grand entry. I suppose it was the first kind of parade I, and lots of other kids, had a chance to ride in.

Most moms packed a good lunch for their crew. I know we were ready for lunch as there were usually a half dozen of us at least that had ridden 12 or so miles to get there.

Back in those days of the Bantry rodeo, I don't think I knew of many famous athletes. I can't think of any big stars like Michael Jordan or Tiger Woods that I idolized at that time. I do know that the Petersons and Brandts were toughs in cow riding and Dale Natwick and Lyle Kramer were calf ropers to watch.

Local celebration brings back memories of the old days

The rodeo was typically long, hot and dusty, but it always seemed too soon when it was over. We usually had to hustle to ride home before dark. Others backed their farm trucks up to the loading chute to load their horses for the trip home. I can remember very few horse trailers at those early Bantry rodeos.

Looking back, it was pretty homespun, even corny, but it was a real event to young kids. Certainly a very important day of the year. It was a celebration of the end of summer, the end of haying, and the start of school the next day.

I did some checking on Labor Day. I was surprised to learn that Labor Day has been around for more than 100 years. Out here on the prairie I suppose it is used more as an excuse to have a holiday than to honor working people, but no matter, lots of places still have Labor Day celebrations.

Labor Day is a big day in Almont. The morning Labor Day parade in Almont is really pretty darn good. There are quite a few horses, several horse drawn wagons and riders always come from neighboring towns. Lots of proud kids riding in probably the only parade they will ever ride in, smiling broadly as they make the trek down main street in Almont.

You'll see some pretty darn nice floats, some really nice old cars and a few surprises in every Labor Day parade. After the parade there is entertainment at the school, a pie and ice cream social, usually a little threshing demonstration, lots of good food and several other activities. The Almont museum is outstanding for a little town and the visitor will be impressed with several Almont businesses open especially for Labor Day.

All of this for the cost of a $1 souvenir Almont Labor Day button. Cheapskates don't even have to buy that.

Labor Day in Almont is somewhat like the old Bantry rodeos. It is pretty homespun, maybe a little corny, but it is a very special day to lots of people.

Up Sims Creek

By: Rod Nelson

Suntans don't get a lot of acknowledgment at Sims

Times are tough here at Sims. Summer is almost a cruel joke. It is over before we even get a chance to do any summer things. People hardly even get a summer look anymore. Only people who run antique machinery like mine, with no cabs, have any color in their face.

Years ago I always used to go without a shirt for awhile and get a real tan. I just seemed to forget about it this summer. There has been a lot of concern recently about ultraviolet rays and the danger of exposure to the sun without using proper sunscreen. It suddenly occurred to me that it was time to get a tan.

Unlike the average tourist, my hot weather garb consists of boots, blue jeans, and most often, long sleeved denim shirts. Seems I can take as much heat as most anyone and don't wear off much hide scratching mosquito bites. For years however, my tan lines were at my neck and at my wrists.

When I announced to my family that I was going to get a tan for health reasons, they were aghast. My daughter especially warned me of the dangers.

"Don't do it, Dad," she pleaded. "What if someone should see you!"

I waited until I was cutting some hay near a road to make my move. I pitched my shirt on the edge of the field, then drove boldly out into the sun.

Even though an older brother and sister of mine have that Howdy Doody hide that flakes off like a molting snake, I wasn't concerned much about burning. I only kept my shirt off for a half hour the first day. Two days later I left it off for a full hour.

It was interesting to watch the traffic on the road. I was darn sure making an impression on some of the drivers. Some of them were visibly shaken by the sight. Several cars almost ran in the ditch. I assumed they hadn't seen so much muscle on a

Suntans don't get a lot of acknowledgment at Sims

man my age. I soon learned I got even more response if I flexed a little when they drove by.

I surprised the family by not burning even a little, like they had predicted I would. My porcelain skin reddened a little, then gradually turned brown. Nothing peeled.

I guess I proved that I could do it, but I'm not sure it was worth it. You get very few accolades here at Sims for suntans.

Until the tan fades away, I have a little proof that summer was here again this year. I don't think that it hurt me. I still think there is more danger in getting too little sun than in getting too much.

Up Sims Creek

By: Rod Nelson

Larry, the Dodge and Tiffany sure enjoyed "the game"

Times are tough here at Sims. I was up near Minot last week looking through my friend Larry's shelterbelt for machinery I could use, when Larry came driving by in his white Dodge pickup.

I was surprised to see that his Dodge looked so beat up. I realized the pickup is not new, but I had always thought it looked pretty good before. I mentioned to Larry that his pickup really seemed to be showing a lot of wear.

Larry acted a little defensive about my comment. He went into a lengthy dialogue about how much work the Dodge had done, talking at length about hauling fuel tanks, making repair runs, hauling fencing materials along rocky pastures and of countless miles pulling loaded livestock trailers, etc. I soon regretted even mentioning his Dodge. It took a while for his testiness to disappear, but soon he seemed to be himself again. It wasn't long until he promised to give me a cultivator to pull in front of the drill he gave me a couple years ago.

I decided to stick around Larry's place for a couple days and help him with the harvest. I have stayed there many times before and know the routine around there well.

This time I couldn't help but notice a change. Mia, a stately old Grand Madame of a dog had passed on and a flea bitten, three-legged Border Collie had taken her place. Larry had an obvious fascination with "Tiffany" and lavished her with attention.

I noticed every time Larry got in his Dodge pickup, Tiffany would drop down, ready to spring away in any direction Larry might go and would race along the Dodge until the pickup left the farmstead.

I didn't think too much of this until one day when I was riding in the Dodge with Larry and Tiffany, as usual, was running in front.

"Watch this!" Larry said, stepping on the gas and turning east towards the haylot.

Larry, the Dodge and Tiffany sure enjoyed "the game"

Tiffany, sensing the change in direction, made a hard left, skirted around some old machinery and bales and tried to head us off.

Larry pulled hard on the wheel and gunned the Dodge, putting it into a slide. It was a marvelous display of driving ability. The Dodge stayed on her wheels as we sped away in a different direction. Larry was pouring the fuel to her, but poor traction in the wet grass allowed Tiffany to temporarily gain the lead.

Tiffany really cruised through the machinery lot, three good legs bounding along with incredible speed, the fourth worthless leg pointing in all directions, but not impeding her speed as she leaped over piles of old machine parts and ran through tall weeds. Larry, now thoroughly engrossed in the race, seemed oblivious to the metallic sounds of old machines going under the wheels of his Dodge.

There are quite a few buildings on the farmstead and we made a few laps around each of them. I am sure neighbors several miles away could see the dust cloud billowing over Larry's shelterbelt that was generated by the spinning wheels of the old Dodge.

When Larry would really get a good lead, he would hide in a building and fall into convulsive laughter as the confused Tiffany would streak by the door looking for him. As soon as she found him they were off again for another run.

I developed a healthy respect for the Dodge as we leaped off little knolls and bottomed out in the holes.

I felt lucky to have survived the game. But the three old friends, Larry, the Dodge and Tiffany, all over-the-hill, seemed to have enjoyed it immensely.

Up Sims Creek

By: Rod Nelson

Prairie fires are almost a North Dakota tradition

Times are tough here at Sims. It's so dry they're finding fish in the Sims Creek with "farmers' lung." It is so dry I am going to pull the shoes off my horses just because of the fire danger (no kidding).

Just a few days ago we had a rather serious fire in the neighborhood caused by a mower bar hitting a rock. The big question is how the fella found grass tall enough to cut in the first place. Anyway, it doesn't take much of a spark to get this tinder-dry grass burning.

Prairie fires are almost a North Dakota tradition. Most stories of North Dakota history make some mention of prairie fires. Most all of us have had to fight prairie fires at some time or another.

If a fella wasn't so darn busy at a fire it would sure be a good place to visit. In grass country, almost everyone who sees the smoke will soon be there. It is a great place to see neighbors and make new acquaintances. The main problem is that it is so hard to visit when you are gasping for breath.

I was really disappointed myself as a firefighter. I didn't have much endurance. A neighbor of mine about 20 years older than me seemed to have about twice the staying power. Every time I thought I had had about enough, I'd look over at Ed still swinging away with his jacket.

I wish I had been better prepared for the fire. All I had to fight fire with was a jacket. The worst thing about the jacket was the fact that it was "my" jacket. Why couldn't it have been a jacket that someone had left in my pickup? Although it may fit my image, I really hate wearing a jacket that has been used for fighting fires.

This jacket had that nice fake wool lining. It really looked nice until you melted most of it. Now it looks more like a cluster of black beads. It doesn't seem to have

Prairie fires are almost a North Dakota tradition

much insulating value anymore and it feels kind of scratchy. It seems to smell kind of funny now, too.

It is hard, especially in this hilly country, to guess just where the fire is burning when you see the smoke. This fire was about five miles away. By the time I knew just where it was, I was too far from home to bring the proper firefighting tools. If I had it to do over again, I would bring the tractor and sprayer that I have sitting in the yard, ready for just such an emergency. A little water in a sprayer can do so much more than a jacket or shirt, however well they are applied. I will bet a three-gallon yard sprayer could put out a pretty fair stretch of fire.

One fella on the line where I was had a common yard rake. You know, the long metal teeth that work good for raking leaves. That was a pretty effective tool. I think it was quite a bit better than my jacket and maybe a little easier to use. At any rate, I think most of us should throw a few things in our vehicles that could be used to fight fire. Things like rakes, shovels, sacks or your favorite firefighting tools. It would be easy to do and might be pretty useful some day.

Pheasant season starts this weekend. A few people who read this story will be heading west to hunt this weekend. As tinder dry as this part of the state is this year, you could very well, despite your best precautions, start a prairie fire. Throw a two or three-gallon yard sprayer filled with water in your vehicle, along with a couple of firefighting tools. You just may save someone a lot of grief.

Up Sims Creek

By: Rod Nelson

Throw caution to the wind – a little trip can be worth it!

Things have been a little too quiet around Sims lately. I told the missus it was time we took a little trip together.

"You mean in the same vehicle and everything?" she asked.

I assured her that I was sincere.

"What are we driving?" was her next question.

I told her we had a choice of my 1981 fencing pickup or her 1987 Mercury Tracer. She elected to offer the use of her vehicle.

She was in quite an uproar preparing for this event. It really soothed her nerves when I promised she wouldn't have to pack any lunches. I assured her that I knew all the best eating places between the Missouri River and the Rocky Mountains.

She fretted quite a bit about the cost of this trip, but I said, "Let's throw caution to the wind and just blow a little cash for once." I told her all she had to worry about was just packing for the journey.

I have been studying a wonderful book lately about the Lewis and Clark Expedition called "Undaunted Courage." I was struck by the similarities in the provisions they packed and what the missus insisted in taking along.

The big day finally arrived and we were off. It was really a treat to drive along with the missus viewing country we had rarely seen together. One of the first scenes was a lovely sight of a prairie creek lined with ash trees ablaze in autumn color.

"What do you think of that?" I asked her.

"It really is beautiful," she said, "but I wonder how the kids are doing without us."

Throw caution to the wind – a little trip can be worth it!

"Oh, they'll be just fine," I assured her. "Just relax and enjoy the trip. Besides, we haven't even gotten past the mailbox yet!"

We got started kind of late, so it wasn't long before we decided we would have to stop and eat in Dickinson. I had promised her we would mingle with high society people like doctors and such, so our first stop would be dinner with Dr. Rowe in Dickinson. Dr. Rowe is one of the best-read people I know. It is rumored that he has the complete collection of the "Far Side" books.

Conveniently enough, Dr. Rowe is the veterinarian at Stockmen's Livestock in Dickinson, so we could eat right there at the sale barn cafe.

Cost-wise we lucked out a bit. Dr. Rowe was out for a minute, so we didn't have to invite him to eat with us. There was only one stool available right away at the lunch counter which I graciously offered to the missus. She had such a good conversation going with the fella on her left that he offered to buy her dinner. Later when the stool on the other side of her became available and I slipped in there, he picked up the tab on my burger as well.

We planned on spending the night in Billings to visit the missus' brother and his wife, but we had lots of time to sight-see on the way. We toured six cities on the way to Billings. I promised we would have all the treats we felt like having. She loved the Coke I bought her at the Shamrock Bar in Wibaux, MT. She enjoyed window shopping at the Cenex convenience store in Glendive. We stopped in Miles City to buy postcards for her friends, but the smog soon forced us out of that town. She was smitten with a second hand store in Forsythe where many of the gifts I have given her for years have come from. She was speechless when I took her out for supper in Hysham's finest cafe.

We rarely do the tourist thing, so we brought a camera along to record all of our

Throw caution to the wind – a little trip can be worth it!

experiences. We soon felt comfortable asking strangers to take our picture in front of all our favorite places. We posed so many times my head felt a little stretched out just from smiling.

After a pleasant visit at the in-laws we were off again. The first thing we discovered the next day was the fact that our camera wasn't working when we left home. We splurged and bought a throw-away camera at a grocery store.

Since this was a once in a lifetime occasion, we decided we wouldn't worry about spending money, we stopped at a wonderful tack shop at Franny, WY, where I got a nice wool vest for myself.

Cody, WY was a blast. We didn't have time to tour the wonderful museum there, but we found a nice shop called Scary Mary's where we bought Halloween masks. We had the absolute best time from then on stopping at gas stations and sitting in the car while people watched us with our masks on. I confess, I wish I had been driving a car that displayed something other than North Dakota license plates.

Riverton, WY puts on an absolutely first class cowboy poetry gathering, so the weekend was lots of fun. I had a nice surprise for the missus in Riverton. The handmade boots I had ordered for myself the year before were done. She must have been pleased. She sure was speechless! I encouraged her to buy a little something for herself, so she spent Saturday morning shopping downtown Riverton. She needed footwear, also, and found a nice pair of boots for $29.

Seemed like all too soon we were on the way home again. We were in quite a lot more of a hurry on the way home, but I stopped to exercise the missus several times: breakfast in Casper, dinner in Belle Fourche and a delightful sandwich at a convenience store in Belfield.

The weekend sure was a success. Sometimes a little trip is well worth the cost!

Up Sims Creek

By: Rod Nelson

It's a sure sign winter's coming when the mice move in

Times are tough here at Sims, but they're not as bad as I thought. I was going to help the missus out of the back seat of the car the other day and as I grabbed her hand I thought to myself, "Wow! This is one old girl who sure could use a little hand lotion." It suddenly dawned on me that she was wearing gloves.

Gloves are just one more sign that the country is cooling off and winter will soon be here.

There are always signs that indicate the season. Years ago a sure sign for late fall was the urge to go trapping. It was almost like a fever to get the traps ready and hit the fields and streams for fur. Most any Christmas money I had for many years was earned from trapping mink or other fur-bearing animals.

I haven't set a trap since I moved to Sims 13 years ago, but that doesn't mean that trapping isn't a sign of fall around our place. We have merely changed roles. The missus runs the traplines these days. You see, this is the time of year when the mice seem to like to move into our house.

Back when I was first married the missus, she would cringe at the sight of a mouse and would beg me to trap them. I would have gladly done this little chore for her, but as I explained to her, "Honey, I don't want you to hold back, even a little, and I don't want to do anything that would keep you from being the 'complete' woman. You will just have to learn how to trap them yourself."

She refused at first, but it wasn't long until she came home well supplied with mouse traps.

She soon became quite proficient at trapping mice. My longtime friend Elizabeth Taylor from Towner was good for giving her trapping tips on trap replacement and proper baits. Liz was a longtime trapper and her advise soon produced good results.

It's a sure sign winter's coming when the mice move in

It is funny how the missus has changed since those days. I can remember when we were first married, sometimes in the middle of the night when a trap would go off under our bed and the mouse would thrash around a bit, the missus would just cringe and I would have to comfort her before she could go back to sleep. Now when she hears the trap go off she bolts straight up in bed, raises a clenched fist and shouts "YES!"

It used to be expensive to have her trapping because she would never reuse a trap. Trap and mouse would both be tossed in the garbage. I am glad she got over her squeamishness about that. Now after she runs her trapline, she may have a fistful of traps when she opens the door and calls, "Here kitty, kitty."

Our mouse problem was compounded several years ago when she killed all the bullsnakes that were living in our basement. I told her not to do it, but she absolutely wouldn't listen. She picked a nice, sunny spring day when they crawled out in the yard to sun themselves. I wasn't home, but the evidence was still draped over the fence when I returned.

I have always wondered what the animal rights people would say about people like the missus.

But I will tell you one thing, as far as the missus is concerned, when it comes to sharing living space, mice and snakes have no rights!

Up Sims Creek

By: Rod Nelson

Long underwear hand-me-downs – a steadfast tradition

Times are tough here at Sims. The calendar shows November but the progress chart shows September. I sure hope that someday I will be truly ready for winter. I am happy, however, that I don't dread winter as much as I used to. Having my very own long underwear has made winter so much nicer.

I still recall that awful day when we were visiting my Aunt Metta and Uncle Jack. I suppose I was about 10 or 11 years old. Metta was telling my Mother about some long woolen underwear of Uncle Jack's that had shrunk "just a bit" in the dryer. "The legs are shrunk up too much for Jack, but I'll bet they would fit Rodney. Would he like some nice, practically new, long underwear?" I signaled frantically to Mom, shaking my head from side to side, rolled my eyes around and around, stuck my tongue out like I was desperately ill, and made choking and gasping sounds. Mom, noting my panic said, "Rodney would love to have some nice new underwear." Metta ran to fetch them and soon returned with about six pairs. I was forced to stand at attention while they held the garments up to me to test them for size. Mom and Metta both agreed that the legs were the perfect length for me. "But Mom," I protested, "the legs are the only thing that shrunk, the waistband goes way too far up." "Oh that won't hurt you," Mom said, "and no one will notice if you keep your shirt buttoned to the top."

When we left that day Mom prodded me in the ribs and said, "What do you say Rodney?" "Gee thanks" I said lamely. "Glad you like them," Uncle Jack said with a broad smile. Uncle Jack was normally somewhat reserved but that day he seemed especially jovial and when I looked back at Jack's farmyard when we got to the main highway I couldn't help but notice Uncle Jack doing backflips out on the driveway.

They were truly "heavy" long underwear. They were as thick as a Navajo saddle blanket and twice as tough. Built before modern science found a way to separate cockleburs from wool, they were as friendly toward skin as coarse sandpaper. They wore like iron.

149

Long underwear hand-me-downs – a steadfast tradition

I will never understand why only the legs shrunk. The top part seemed enormous. There was no strolling around the house wearing just the underwear unless I wore them with suspenders. There was no denying that they kept my legs warm but dealing with the top part was a real problem. I had to tuck the top into my pants as best as I could. I was the only 75 pound fifth grader with severe midriff bulge.

Looking back, I find it difficult to believe that Uncle Jack was the first owner of these underwear. I'll bet he inherited them from an uncle of his, perhaps a sumo wrestler. They had the deepest crotch of any garment I have ever seen. When I reached six feet in height I told Mom I had to get some new underwear. "What is wrong with your Uncle Jack's underwear?" she asked. When I claimed they didn't fit she held them up to me and noted that they reached perfectly from my waist to my ankles. The fact that the crotch reached below my knees didn't seem to bother her at all.

I finally grew enough so the top became almost manageable. I probably wouldn't have minded them if I could have found a pair of socks long enough to reach high enough to overlap the bottom of the legs. Long underwear that don't reach the knee just don't cut it.

They never wore out. I always hoped someone would give me a gift of nice long underwear, but no one ever did. I didn't get new long underwear for high school graduation. I didn't get any for college graduation. I suppose if the missus hadn't snickered so much on our wedding night I'd still be wearing them. It was hard to throw clothing away that was in such good condition but I did. It was sure stupid of me to toss them. I have a few nephews that could have sure used them!

Up Sims Creek

By: Rod Nelson

Christmas shopping just isn't as easy as it used to be

Times are tough here at Sims. My Christmas shopping list is longer than my bank account. In an effort to save a little money I decided to start shopping before December 24 for the first time in my life.

I used to enjoy shopping a lot more than I do now. Years ago you could drive into any small town and do your shopping. Small town shopping was the best ever. I remember walking into Busch's department store in Towner, at three o'clock on December 24 and handing Marilyn my shopping list. No, the list didn't say socks, shirts or handkerchiefs. It said, "Mom and Dad, Cody, Todd, Chris, Cari, and Susie," and so on. Marilyn, in feigned, or perhaps genuine, exasperation would give me a three-minute tongue lashing and then would fly into action. "How old is Cody now?" she'd ask, heading into the kid's department. "Do your nieces like to wear dresses? Would Martha like a new housecoat?" "You're the doctor," I'd say lamely. "Take all the time you need Marilyn, but hurry every chance you get."

Within an hour I'd leave the store, my shopping finished and every package wrapped. I'd leave satisfied and refreshed. Sometimes I'd even have time to visit with the paramedics as they came to treat Marilyn.

Back in those days if I really was in the mood to shop I'd go to Minot. Minot, before shopping malls, was a great place to shop. Downtown Minot was ablaze with Christmas lights and filled you with the Christmas spirit. You could usually find a parking place within one block of downtown Minot. Every store in Minot that counted could be found in the downtown area.

Woolworth's was a great place to go. Called the "Dime Store" at that time, it filled the needs of the financially impaired. There was a great soda fountain there and best of all, an escalator. I'll admit I spent many an hour riding up and down on that escalator. It was a great time unless there was a bunch of snot-nosed city kids riding on it too. I used to hate it when they would say things like. "Why don't you go back to the country and watch TV with your wife," or something like that.

Christmas shopping just isn't as easy as it used to be

The best thing about shopping then was the nice neat stores. Penny's for example, had everything that Penny's stores have now, but it was nice and compact. Shirts, underwear, socks all came in neat packages and could be found in nice, little pidgeon holes in a certain part of the store. I'll bet the whole men's department in the old Minot Penny's store would fit in just the handkerchief department of the Penny,s store in Bismarck today. It would be a great place to calve out a bunch of heifers, but I sure hate shopping there.

All of the modern shopping malls seem to contain a lot of huge stores with different names but the same bland merchandise. The main choice is weather to buy something made in Bangladesh, Korea, or China. These stores are usually about one heart attack apart and the territory in between is jammed with crazed shoppers and packs of roving mall walkers.

The modern stores are so big you have to look up high to check for signs that tell you where to go. Country people are used to taking a straight line to their destination. This can get you in trouble. Take for instance those times when you are shopping for the missus. You have just been to the Lawn and Garden section and made a purchase. Across the store you see a sign that reads "Housewares." You get halfway there and all of a sudden the new rake you purchased gets hung up in a rack of women's lingerie. You can thrash around in there like a coyote in a trap until some haughty sales lady helps you out.

Those lingerie departments make me nervous anyway. It's no wonder so many women get colds in the winter! I can't imagine how women use a lot of that stuff. Most western tack shops have less straps and buckles. By the looks of some of that stuff it must be used for mosquito netting or something.

The last good store I know of is the Farm and Home in Bismarck. Most everything you need is crammed high on shelves in tight little aisles. I see they are building a new store. Good, easy shopping will soon be a thing of the past.

Up Sims Creek

By: Rod Nelson

Christmas on the Prairie

If you'd never heard the radio
or had never been to town,
you'd still know it on the prairie
when Christmas rolls around.

It's not easy to explain it,
but the prairie lets you know
it's more than just the winter wind,
the ice and drifting snow.

There's a feeling like a shiver,
it's like music to your ear.
The prairie radiates it
at this certain time of year.

If you go out on the prairie
on a clear and starlit night,
it can almost leave you breathless
just to view the awesome sight.

Out here you need no mountains
to get you feeling high
'cause way out on the prairie
you can almost touch the sky.

If you listen, really listen,
and believe with all your might,
you can sometimes hear the sleigh bells
as they tinkle in the night.

And out on the horizon
you see reindeer and a sleigh.
You can see old Santa coming
from a hundred miles away.

Or if you stand in silence
and absorb that awesome view,
waves of former Christmases
come rolling in to you.

The frost might freeze your fingers
or send shivers up your hide,
but the warmth of Christmas memories
makes you glow, and glow inside.

It kinda makes you humble
and it seems hard to believe
the same stars shining brightly
shone on that first Christmas eve.

There's a place for all that tinsel
and those artificial lights,
but they just can't match the splendor
of those prairie winter nights.

The natural decorations
kindle warmth down in your soul.
It's ablaze in all its splendor
from Sims to the North Pole.

153

Christmas on the Prairie

And the prairie lets you see it
so clearly and so true.
There's no buildings, trees,
  or mountains
to muddle up the view.

They can have their city sidewalks
or the mountains to the west.
But way out on the prairie –
that's where Christmas is the best!

Up Sims Creek

By: Rod Nelson

Being older allows one to take a crack at weather forecasting

Times are tough here at Sims. Finally have beautiful winter grazing weather and no grass.

Do have some feed tho and its nice to see the feed make some condition on those old cows instead of just going up in steam.

Good winter feed in mild weather makes for good condition on livestock. If you don't believe me just step on the scale after being on self-feeders through the holiday season!

Seems like Christmas is here all the time since old age has struck. I always heard time goes faster and faster the older you get. Old age is supposed to bring wisdom. I don't know if that is true or not but I do feel I am finally old enough to take a crack at weather forecasting.

Here is my forecast for North Dakota and surrounding states for 1998.

January will finally bring some winter-like weather to our parts. We will see several overnight lows of -10 degrees to -20 degrees. We need these temperatures just to feel right about living so far north. These low temperatures will come on days with little or no wind. It will warm up above zero during the day every day through January. The rest of January will be much like the weather we have enjoyed in December. The last week of January will be really warm. Many people who think they look good in shorts will be wearing them. Many people who know better will have to see them.

Look for a pleasant February until about the 20th. We should have a proper winter storm blowing through about that time. Kids will get a one-day break from school. People who have invested money in snow equipment will get a chance to try it out. Don't dig out too quick tho. Daytime highs in the 20's will soon return.

March will come in like a lamb. Expect balmy temperatures until about March 6th when precipitation rolls in. March 6th through 9th should bring heavy snow.

155

Being older allows one to take a crack at weather forecasting

Accumulations will run from 20-24 inches. This will hardly be a storm as winds will be light. Mid-March will bring daily highs in the 40 degree range. All snow will be melted by March 20. Runoff will be slight to none. March will go out like a lamb.

April will be warm and dry. In early April farmers will be working all night. Ranchers who aren't worried about calving problems will sleep through the night.

April 20th should bring about an inch of rain to most of the area. Temperatures will rise to the 70 degree range within a day.

Grass should be grand by May 7th. If farmers want to get a crop they better have everything planted by May 10th. The last 20 days in May will be wet. Memorial Day weekend will start with heavy rain changing to brilliant sunshine and highs in the 80's.

Look for cool nights and pleasant warm days in June. Western North Dakota should see about one inch of rain per week. The Devils Lake region will see scant but adequate precipitation. June 20th through 30th should be dry and warm.

July 1st and 2nd should bring lots of precipitation. It will still be muddy enough on July 4th so you can do little but celebrate.

July will be fairly dry after the 4th. Look for a good rain about the 20th and 29th.

August will bring some real summer weather. Other than a good soaker about the 15th, it should be warm and dry. Highest temperature will be about August 24th of about 92 degrees.

September should bring about a week of drizzle starting on the 15th. Other than creating a lot of misery for boxelder bugs, it won't be too bad. The last few days of September will bring a lot of moisture to most of the area.

Being older allows one to take a crack at weather forecasting

Goose hunters will curse October weather. Geese won't even think of coming to North Dakota until November.

Mid November will bring a winter storm with enough wind to finally blow the autumn colors off the trees. Look for a warming trend after that which will melt the snow.

December of 1998 will be much like 1997. The main difference will be about four inches of snow on the 23rd of December. Don't know yet about '99. Too early to tell. Happy New Year!

Up Sims Creek

By: Rod Nelson

Roy Rogers couldn't shoot well, but he sure could ride!

Times are tough here at Sims. Have had cold feet for the first time in years. Wish it would snow a little so it would be worthwhile to wear overshoes.

Darn long winter evenings make a fella wonder what to do sometimes. Once in awhile I can't seem to find a book that suits me and I have to dig around for some other kind of entertainment. The kids have quite a few movies stashed around the place and we dig one of them out now and then. We seem to have quite a few Roy Rogers movies and we watch them occasionally.

Back when I was a kid, Roy Rogers was very popular. I don't remember if I ever went to a Roy Rogers movie, but I suppose I did. I do remember watching the Roy Rogers show on TV.

Even though Roy Rogers was a national kids' hero at that time, I don't think we thought all that much of him. As a ranch-raised kid, I think Roy seemed a little phony with his fancy, fringed shirts and pants tucked in those fancy little boot tops.

Cowboy heroes for us were North Dakota cowboys like Duane Howard, Joe Chase, Alvin Nelson and the Teschers. We knew they were for real. If we got to go to one of the big rodeos like the Minot indoor or the Mandan Fourth of July Rodeo we could see them ride.

It seems funny, forty years later to look at Roy Rogers in a different way.

I really get a kick out of seeing Roy Rogers movies now. Yes, I know most of the acting isn't the greatest and most of it still looks pretty phony, but I am really impressed with Roy Rogers as a horseman.

Most cowboys have a built-in aversion to palomino horses, but old Trigger was a pretty good horse. A couple of years ago I had a chance to go to the Roy Rogers Museum in Victorville, California and I got to see Trigger. He looked as good as a

Roy Rogers couldn't shoot well, but he sure could ride!

taxidermist could make him. I noticed he wasn't all that big. If I remember right they showed him in a rearing position. I doubt if he was 15 hands, but then Roy was a pretty small man as well. I know he didn't look nearly as impressive there as he did in the movies.

I would kill to have a Blue Heeler trained as well as old Trigger. He could do just about anything. It would be fun to spend some time with the guy who trained him, but no matter what level of training he had, he couldn't have looked so good without a good hand on his back.

I am more and more impressed with Roy's ability to ride.

If you watch a typical chase scene in a Roy Rogers movie, Trigger is always the fastest horse. Sometimes they cross some pretty rough terrain, but I am pretty sure it is Roy, not a stuntman in the saddle. Roy never bounces around. He is stuck to old Triggers' back like glue.

That is true, blazing down the road, jumping logs, or just spinning old Trigger around.

It is beautiful to watch Roy run and jump up on Trigger. He had the most impressive way of jumping up and hitting the stirrups with perfect precision. He could also make some nice jumps off of rocks or buildings onto Trigger's back. I'll bet there were times when they had to do a retake but who knows. I have never seen any videos of Roy Rogers Bloopers for sale.

It impresses me to think that they could take a guy noted for his singing ability and make a movie cowboy out of him. Can you imagine a runaway stage coach scene with Garth Brooks, Willie Nelson, or the Kentucky Head Hunters riding in pursuit?

One thing about old Roy that doesn't impress me is his shooting ability. He can burn up more ammo and hit less that anyone I know. He should have shooting

Roy Rogers couldn't shoot well, but he sure could ride!

lessons from the same guy that trained Clint Eastwood. I know Tom Tescher could outshoot him any day of the week.

Anyway, I have learned to respect Roy more and more for the things I didn't notice when I was a kid. I'm not kiddin' when I say I enjoy seeing his movies. Besides, they are among the few movies the missus will let me watch!

Up Sims Creek

By: Rod Nelson

Unlucky enough to receive the "lucky" chain letter...

Times are tough here at Sims. Seems like I never really get lucky. Some people seem to be lucky all the time, while others seem to have a black cloud hovering over them. Of course, there are always some people who seem to have more bad luck than I do, but it would be nice to really hit the jackpot sometime.

A few days ago when I stopped and picked up the mail, one letter kind of jumped out at me. There was no return address, but it looked like a nice personal letter to me. At any rate, it looked more appealing than the average bill, so I opened it as I drove into the yard. I soon realized I had received this letter, or letters like it, in the past.

This paper has been sent to you for good luck. The original is in England. It has been around the world nine times. You will receive good luck within four days of receiving this letter, provided you, in turn, send it on...

The letter then went on, in typical fashion, relating tales of people who received such great luck after receiving this letter, and gave accounts of the dreadful consequences of not sending the chain letter on to twenty people within four days.

I couldn't help but feel disdain for the person who had sent me this mindless drivel. What kind of a spineless, superstitious wimp would believe that trash enough to actually send it on, I thought, as I parked my pickup by my barn door and walked inside to turn some horses out. I had received these letters before and had faithfully trashed each and every one of them.

The letter stayed on my mind for the few minutes it took me to care for the horses. It was still on my mind when I went back outside to get back in my pickup. The pickup was gone! What a stroke of bad luck to forget to set the parking brake! Worse yet, the pickup was about 100 yards away right up against my gooseneck trailer.

I walked down to my pickup fearing the worst. I expected to see a smashed bumper and was certain that the trailer would be smashed badly. Miraculously, the pickup had stopped within inches of my trailer, hurting nothing.

Unlucky enough to receive the "lucky" chain letter . . .

Later that day I was driving my new 1989 Olds with 130,000 miles on it. I was thinking how lucky I was that I was able to pay so little for such a good old car when the engine started missing badly. It seemed pretty bad until I topped the hill, then it started running smoothly again. "Wow! That was a stroke of good luck," I thought. "Must have been just a little dirt in the fuel or something." I stopped in Almont to do a couple of errands and then left for Dickinson. The Olds hummed up the Curlew Valley like a well-tuned watch.

"Rats!" A couple of miles east of Glen Ullin, my alternator light came on. I cursed my bad luck and almost decided to drive up to I-94 and drive on to Dickinson, but better judgment told me to drive in to Glen Ullin. The Olds quit on me right at the door of Duane's Motor Service. I had to admit that as bad as it was to have the alternator go out, it was certainly good luck to have it quit right at the mechanic's door in the middle of the afternoon. Duane told me the bad news and the good news. The bad news was the alternator was not repairable and quite expensive to replace. The good news was that the NAPA dealer in Glen Ullin had one in stock. Duane stopped what he was doing, drove over and got the alternator, and replaced it for me. In only small-town fashion, he didn't charge me anything for the labor as it didn't take very long.

Within a few minutes, I was back on the road heading for Dickinson. I couldn't help but think how lucky I was that the alternator chose such a good time and place to go on the blink.

The chain letter stated that I would have to send it on within 96 hours. After a couple of days I got to thinking that I should send it on, just for the fun of it. It may be fun to report how much my luck continued to change.

Unlucky enough to receive the "lucky" chain letter . . .

There was no way I would ask anyone to copy the letter for me as I knew that would make me feel foolish, but I thought I could type it on my computer and make 20 copies. Lo and behold, my printer was completely out of paper! It was then I realized the letter probably did bring luck. I saved twenty envelopes, twenty sheets of paper and $6.40 in postage, and twenty other people were lucky enough to have not received this drivel in their mail!

Up Sims Creek

By: Rod Nelson

Fashion and style are all in the eyes of the beholder

Times are tough here at Sims. The only way I can forget my troubles is to wear badly fitting boots.

I hate to wear poor boots. Being cursed with #12AA feet, I have worn lots of badly fitting boots through the years. I finally have learned that the good ones are worth the money. The hard part is to order them without the missus finding out about it and facing her a year later when the boots finally are delivered.

I don't order fancy boots. I pass up the fancy options. I just try to order quality. Sometimes I get it and sometimes I am deceived. The last pair of boots I got, why, even the missus thought they looked plain.

I can spot good boots at a glance. Most people probably would miss some of the signs. Many boots that people think look stylish, I think look amazingly bad. If I see anything made from dead snakes or chickens I am never impressed.

I have never been known to be a very stylish dresser, and only the few people who have the same kind of foot problems as I do notice the boots I wear, and make any comments about them.

Lots of people put great emphasis on style. The tag on the clothing is more important than the garment itself. Many people want to shop only in a fashionable place like the GAP. The GAP means nothing to me. I have lots of clothing that have gaps. Seems like it gets easier all the time to buy clothing that soon has gaps. I dislike gaps.

Most fashionable clothing has little value to me. For example, "Polar King" is of much more importance to me on my place than "Armani."

I can smell the stores that I like. Duck hunters and loggers like many of the same

Fashion and style are all in the eyes of the beholder

waterproof and durable brands of clothing that I like. Brand names like "Filson" or "Pendleton" always get my attention. Even though I usually can't afford to buy a lot of those brands of clothing, I appreciate them for their quality, durability, and yes, even their usually simple style.

The trouble with wearing those types of clothing, you usually wind up wearing them until you get sick of them, or other people get sick of them.

I have a decent Pendleton jacket that I guess I have had for quite awhile.

A couple of weeks ago at the National Cowboy Poetry Gathering in Elko I visited with a man from a large Utah city. I remember him from other years. He had been very nice and complimentary to me and asked me for permission to use a couple of my poems in an upcoming poetry contest. He was dressed impeccably, in proper "buckaroo" attire. One glance at him and I could tell he knew nothing about horses, cattle or anything associated with ranching or cowboys. I liked the guy anyway, and was happy to give him permission to use any of my poems. We ran into each other several times in the next couple of days and exchanged pleasantries. Curiosity finally got the best of him and pointing at my old Pendleton he asked, "Say, is that the only jacket you own?"

It seemed like a strange comment to me who can't help but feel that a garment is like a pickup. The more miles I get out of it, the better I like it.

I suppose I am a little style-conscious when it comes to blue jeans. Any more, I won't wear anything but Wranglers. I don't think they wear any better than any thing else, but I like them and think any other brand looks plain bad! I have seen blue jeans in places like Saks Fifth Avenue that I wouldn't be caught dead in, even if I could afford to pay the ridiculous price they had on them. If someone had asked me who Calvin Klein was a few years ago, I suppose I would have guessed he was

Fashion and style are all in the eyes of the beholder

just another farm boy from the German-Russian triangle in North Dakota. I have since learned that Calvin Klein is a brand name that deserves respect. I still wouldn't wear a pair of Calvin Klein jeans.

A couple of weeks ago my brother-in-law from Billings came to visit. He gave me two pair of Calvin Klein briefs. I told him that I had quit wearing used underwear. He told me that he had bought a three-pack, had worn one pair, didn't like the fit, and was giving me the other two pair. My brother-in-law is a fine, decent man, but he is still wearing the 1968 model suit he graduated from high school in and I was somewhat suspicious. I had the sneaking suspicion that Calvin Klein underwear came in a two-pack, but I grudgingly accepted them.

I wore them to a wedding that night. Since I was finally wearing something I assumed was fashionable I was feeling quite smug. The photographer asked me that evening if I would like to have my picture taken. I thought I was being clever when I said, "I really should pose for you in my new shorts, they are Calvin Klein's, you know." "Really," she said, "What is he wearing?"

Up Sims Creek

By: Rod Nelson

North Dakota Olympics would be an event to remember

Things have been picking up here at Sims. We have really been tuned in to the Olympics for the last couple of weeks. It is nice to look at our TV, see snow, and know that it is supposed to be there.

I really enjoy the Winter Olympics. It's easier for those of us from the Northern Plains to relate to than the Summer Olympics, although there are a couple of things I would change. I would like to see less emphasis on all that figure skating. I get sick of grown men sobbing every time they lose. They ought to try ranching some time.

At any rate, it is always sad to see the Olympics come to an end. I was bemoaning this fact when all at once an idea came to mind. Why not have a North Dakota Winter Olympics? This could be an invitational celebrity Olympics featuring our most recognized North Dakotans. I suppose we could invite celebrity teams from South Dakota, Minnesota, Montana, Manitoba and Saskatchewan. This could become a major event!

Choosing the site for this event should be easy. The logical place would be Sims. The east side of Sims hill is steep enough for all the skiing and bobsledding events. I suppose the lack of snow may concern some, but I am sure all you would need would be some frost on the grass for optimum speed.

Speed skating couldn't be better than on I-94. We could run a few water trucks up the highway on a cold day and soon have a proper track. Straightaway skating races would be held east to west, against the wind for the optimum challenge.

Cross-country skiing courses would be a snap to make. Lots of open country with rolling hills around here. It could be set up so spectators could all sit on a vantage point and be able to see almost the whole race. It would be grand seeing the competitors speeding down the north slopes on snow, viewing the crashes as they hit bare ground on the bottom and sprinting with their skis to the next patch of snow.

North Dakota Olympics would be an event to remember

We may have to move to the Missouri River for the figure skating and ice dancing competitions. It would be interesting to see the competitors skate on less than perfectly smooth ice. An added bonus would be the river banks that spectators could sit on.

We could use most of the regular Olympic events, but they could be altered somewhat to fit North Dakota conditions. For instance, the Biathlon could be changed from skiing and shooting rifles to perhaps a somewhat different format. Competitors could don heavy coveralls and four-buckle overshoes. Contestants would have to chase pregnant cows into a barn on foot. Extra points would be awarded for accurate hits with frozen cow turds.

We are a little short on celebrities here in North Dakota, but I think we could get enough people to make it interesting.

Folk singer Chuck Suchy would be a logical choice for long-distance speedskating.

Governor Schafer no doubt would be a fierce competitor in the giant slalom.

Former Governor Art Link would be my pick to captain the four-man bobsled team.

Dr. Rowe of Dickinson, by his own admission, the top veterinarian in North Dakota and also a noted long-distance runner, would be a top candidate for the 30K cross country skiing race. He could also double as the team doctor.

I am not sure who we could use for the long-distance ski jumping competition, but I am leaning toward former bull rider Duane Howard. I think they still may have a ski jumping place near Devils Lake where he could practice, and after all the bulls and broncs Duane has seen, I don't think ski jumping would intimidate him.

For the two-man luge, I would go with Earl Pomeroy and Milo Hatzenbuhler.

North Dakota Olympics would be an event to remember

Sarah Vogel would be interesting in freestyle aerials.

I like the image of champion bronc rider Brad Gjermundson ice dancing, cheek to cheek, to a dreamy waltz with Heidi Heitkamp.

Any politicians that we aren't sure what to do with could certainly find a place on our hockey team. I think this Olympics would put North Dakota on the map and certainly would be an Olympics to remember.

If it goes through, I'll look forward to seeing you at the Olympic Village in Almont!

Up Sims Creek

By: Rod Nelson

God made a few perfect heads, the rest he covered with hair . . .

Times are tough here at Sims. Can't even have dandruff any more. There's just no place to put the stuff.

I was looking at a picture of Great Grandpa Charles Johnson the other day. It just isn't fair! If I had to inherit the baldness trait, I should have at least inherited the trait to grow hair on my face. I really don't miss hair all that much except that it is so darn painful when you bump your head, and probably the worst thing about baldness is the fact that it is so darn hot. You would think that it would be cool, but it isn't. Hair gets wet and evaporates, cooling your head, but a bald head heats up like leather seats in a Cadillac parked in the sun. The only good thing is that the heat constantly shrinks the hide on the top of your head, which takes the slack out of your face. That is why bald men are so much better looking than those with lots of hair. You don't believe me! Just look around. Find an old fella that is really proud of his nice wavy hair and nine times out of ten, you'll find enough loose hide hanging under his chin to make a suitcase.

From the comfort point of view, I wouldn't mind having hair, but I'd hate to sacrifice that "macho" look that comes with baldness. It seems strange to me that many bald men actually try to conceal their baldness. We all know lots of men who think they can hide their baldness by dragging some neck hair up and across their head. It's about as effective as trying to tarp a truck with a gymnast's drawers.

I suppose there are a lot of bald men who just have gotten too tired of all the attention a bald head gets. A stranger whose best tooth looks like a seventy-year-old cedar post will think nothing of telling you the worn out Preparation H story right in the middle of a reception line at a wedding. Walk around anywhere without a hat and people will be shading their eyes and moaning something about needing sunglasses for the glare. One can only assume jealousy!

Men would do better to draw attention to their baldness rather than away from it. A couple of days ago I was standing in a line and glanced down at the fella in front of

God made a few perfect heads, the rest he covered with hair . . .

me. I almost jumped when I looked down at his bald head and noticed a pair of eyes staring at me. He had a couple of big, wide-open eyes tattooed on the back of his head!

Ordinarily I am not too big on tattoos, although they seem to be gaining more popularity all the time. The current rage seems to be ankle tattoos for women. That one I can't figure out. There are plenty of ankles that don't need any attention drawn to them, but you still won't see a bald man walk up to a lady in a shopping mall and say something like, "Hey lady, if you put that tattoo on your nose, maybe people wouldn't notice your legs! Ha Ha!"

I will admit though, that the eyes tattooed on the back of that fella's head did intrigue me. Endless possibilities started popping into my mind. Men with really bad hairpieces could just get their heads tattooed. It could look as real as artificial turf. You could have any kind of hair you wanted tattooed on your head and never have to worry about cutting, combing, or washing the stuff. I am sure you could have a straight or wavy look in any color you'd desire and it would never fall out or turn gray. I am sure if you really wanted realism you could even get some dandruff flecks tattooed in there as well. I could, however, see some problems getting the tattooed hair to look as if it was standing on end.

Maybe a fella would like to use the tattoos for a more practical purpose. Guys with a real round head could have the top part of the globe tattooed on. Some could only get Canada on but others I am sure could get at least to South Dakota. Flat headed guys could get a checkerboard tattoo. Think of all the fun the grandchildren could have! The top of a head would be a great place to record important telephone numbers and pertinent lists. It would be easier to access the information stored on the top of your head that to power up the computer. I suppose the big drawback would be another dose of inferiority complex for the hairy-headed guys.

I think I'll leave my head natural. I'm getting plenty of attention the way it is!

Up Sims Creek

By: Rod Nelson

The wife earns the income, but the husband creates the refund!

Times are tough here at Sims. 1997 was such a bad year that I hated to do my taxes, because I didn't want to be reminded of it.

Didn't get started on my 1997 record book until after the tax filing deadline. Lucked out a little when they extended the deadline on account of that big blizzard. I guess the IRS doesn't have to know that the storm didn't hit Sims.

I still have a fella up in Minot do my taxes, I really should find someone closer to do the task, but I'd hate to have any more people know how bad a shape I'm in.

Doing taxes seemed to be easier years ago. I know they must have been easier for my Dad anyway. Other than answer some of Mom's questions, he didn't have much to do with it. Mom would wrestle with the pile of canceled checks for a couple of days and it was over for another year.

I don't remember many people having to pay much in income taxes back then and there aren't many years when ranchers have to pay income taxes now either. The big problem now days concerns the income tax refunds.

Years ago, there were no tax refunds to worry about because no one had any taxes withheld during the year. That is no longer the case. On modern farms and ranches, the wife most often has an off-the-farm job. Most rural women are no longer contented with staying out in the sticks like they used to be. They seem to enjoy getting out into the workplace, using their talents, and probably enjoy the camaraderie of the workplace as well. It is not like they need to work. Modern rural women like to spend their earnings on frivolous things like food, clothing, and utilities. Modern rural men spend their earnings on essentials like repairs, rent, interest, fuel, vet bills, etc.

The wife earns the income, but the husband creates the refund!

Tax-time has created some major problems in rural America because a lot of modern women think they are entitled to their own tax refund!

At a quick glance, a lot of people would tend to side with the women. It would seem to make sense to the casual observer that the one who paid the taxes should have the refund, however, it doesn't take a genius to see that the husband has made the refund possible. Without him, there would be no refund. Without the husband's input the money would actually go to taxes. It would be spent on all the foolish things that the government spends things on.

Sure, the ladies work hard for the money, but the husband has to make many critical decisions that make the refund possible. The old boy may have made a brilliant decision to feed the calves an extra three months during a period of declining cattle prices. Perhaps he rented some extra land, spared no expense to go for the maximum yields, and had the good fortune to hit a drought year. He may have made some well-timed investments in vehicles or machinery to make the refund possible.

Let's say the woman does get the refund. Nine times out of ten she'll spend it foolishly on something like your children's teeth, a new railing on the porch step, or gravel for the driveway.

If you let the husband have the refund, you can bet your life that he'll spend it on something that will make a refund possible next year!

Up Sims Creek

By: Rod Nelson

Iditarod race produces local, modern-day hero

Things are picking up here at Sims. I've been needing a new hero for a long time and I finally got one. His name is Brad Pozarnsky and he is from Bottineau.

I don't know much about Brad Pozarnsky. Never met the fella. Never talked to him on the phone. Haven't read much about him. Doubt if he is a cowboy. He could be one, but I don't know. Don't know if he is doctor or lawyer or if he makes an honest living.

Couldn't tell you if he is a farmer or rancher and if he is I wouldn't have a clue if he fixes his fences, brags too much about his yields, lies about his weaning weights, drives a Rambler car or a Moline tractor.

Don't know if he is a boring conversationalist. Don't know if he takes a bath once a week. Don't know what church he goes to or if he goes to church. If he does go to church, I don't know if he sleeps, makes disgusting sounds, or gives the preacher his undivided attention.

Don't know if he is a North Dakota native. Don't know if he has bad breath, can't dance or thinks Rush Limbaugh is clever. Don't know if he can spell Rush Limbaugh.

Don't know if he has children. If he does have children, I don't know if they lay around in the house on Saturdays and watch TV or play mindless games on computers. Don't know if they are polite, ambitious, or treat old folks with respect. Don't know if they help with chores without complaint.

I heard he is married, but I couldn't tell you if he hugs his wife, tells her she's cute, or buys her lots of presents.

If I could make some assumptions, I would say that I doubt if Brad Pozarnsky snivels about snow, cold weather, or North Dakota winters unless they are too dry and warm. I doubt if Brad Pozarnsky is a vegetarian or an animal rights activist. By the sound of his name, I would guess he is a darn poor Norwegian. If I were to

Iditarod race produces local, modern-day hero

guess, and don't tell me if I'm wrong, that Brad is a pretty decent kind of guy.

About all I could tell you about Brad Pozarnsky is that he entered the Iditarod, he showed up and he finished last. That is at least three remarkable feats.

Just to have guts enough to enter is something. To have a vehicle good enough to make it clear to Alaska with all that equipment and all those dogs is impressive. To finish an 1150-mile dog sled race is a tremendous accomplishment.

I understand that his goal was to finish. He did that. Like I say, to have the gumption to enter is more than most of us will ever have. He finished the race. He finished in last place, but the time he ran the race in would have been good enough to win several past Iditarod races.

I would rather finish the Iditarod than weigh less than Oprah!

Can you imagine the hardship of driving a team of dogs that distance. I have read enough about the race to know that it takes remarkable endurance, unbelievable hard work, and courage to finish.

For those of us who couldn't teach a dog to sit, stay, or pee on a tire, the thought of teaching something like sixteen or so dogs to pull a sled in the direction we want to go for that distance is mind boggling.

Don't know if Brad has a pot to pee in or a window to throw it out of, but I know he finished the Iditarod.

Someday when Brad is sharing space in the Bottineau nursing home with retired bankers, lawyers, farmers, teachers or whomever, people will point to him and say, "See that old fella over there? That's Brad Pozarnsky. He once run the Iditarod!"

Up Sims Creek

By: Rod Nelson

The Elevator Scale By: Rod Nelson
Ask any rancher: There are certain limits to record keeping

Now don't blame me
   the blame should fall
on the guilty I'd insist.
the one who caused the grief for me
was that Ag economist.

He said my style was obsolete
and that mode no longer pays.
If I wished to stay in business
I must yield to modern ways.

I must keep records every day
despite the mental pain.
I should calculate my feed costs
know my cattles' rate of gain.

Well the figures I collected
they could drive sane men berserk.
took the pleasure out of ranching
and it doubled all my work.

We measured something every day
like what every critter ate.
Beauty wouldn't save a brood cow
if her EPD's weren't great.

Then we frame sized all the chickens
and we speed bred all the cats.
and to maximize production
kept Blue Heeler biting stats.

Records now became a passion.
Nothing else was now much fun.
Everything I had was measured
that is all of them but one!

Well, I didn't want to do it.
What else am I to say?
I started up my pickup truck
and loaded it with hay.

I never had a clue that morn
that what I did was wrong.
when I stopped and asked the missus
if she'd like to come along.

She inquired of my intentions
I'll admit I lied that day.
"Well I'm going to New Salem
just to weigh this load of hay.

The Elevator Scale By: Rod Nelson
Ask any rancher: There are certain limits to record keeping

I checked the readout on the scale
as I drove up with my bride.
then I told her sweet as sugar
that she'd have to step outside.

She hesitated not a bit
why she even acted glad.
It was when I checked the scale again
that she knew that she'd been had.

Have you ever known the fury
of a hundred rabid dogs?
Or been in a metal building
when they're castrating hogs?

OH you should have heard
    the screaming
and you should have heard her wail.
The day I weighed the missus
On the elevator scale!

Up Sims Creek

By: Rod Nelson

Although they're great to have, computers are just machines

Times are tough here at Sims. I have been needing a different tractor so have been watching the auction bills hoping to find the tractor of my dreams. Trouble is, all the farmers going broke have better equipment than I can afford!

Machines were designed to make less work for people. I bought a computer hoping that it would make record-keeping easier. The longer I have the thing, the more use I get out of it. E-mail is kind of nice and fun as well. I communicate with people that I wouldn't normally write to on a regular basis.

I received an e-mail message from a cousin a couple of weeks ago. He had just gotten a computer and was learning how to use it. He was excited about possible ways he could benefit from using his new machine. One comment of his stuck in my mind. He said, "Now is not the time to be a Luddite."

It struck me when I realized that I have Luddite tendencies. I do appreciate what machines can do for me, but I really don't like machines. I can operate machines, but they better not break down. I can operate machinery, but hate to start it, hook it up, or fix the stuff. A good machine to me is one that requires little or no maintenance.

I thought I would like the computer because it didn't have any grease zerks, dipsticks, drawbars, filters or fuel tanks on it. I expected it to operate with no problems. I have since learned that computers are still machines. Sometimes it will lock up solid, sometimes it acts up, and sometimes it does a poor job.

I liked the ease of sending my column to the Farm and Ranch Guide. Type it up, follow a few small steps, hit the fax button and it was there. I faxed it in for quite a while, then learned it was easier for those in the office if I e-mailed the column.

Two weeks ago I sat down to write the column, thought I was too tired, and decided to e-mail a poem of mine instead of writing something new. I was surprised when I saw the poem in the paper. Machinery had let me down again! All that reached the

Although they're great to have, computers are just machines

office was the left column of the poem. Only half of it, the first half. I sure thought it looked funny without the good half of the poem included. Strangely enough, several people who had never mentioned my column before, complimented me on the poem.

One thing about the computer that I really liked was that all the columns I had written were on the computer, to be viewed or printed as I wished. Backup discs were of no concern to me. A year ago I learned that computers, like horses, can be struck by lightning. Bye-bye two years of columns.

I do really appreciate some of my labor saving machinery, like plastic feed pails for instance. They are so much lighter than the old steel grease pails we used to use. And who would like to go back to the old TV sets that you used to have to walk up to and change the channel with a knob. The TV remote saves a lot of work and besides that, if you are the one with the remote in hand, you experience the joy of power over your household.

To me, a cow is a great labor-saving machine. The cow walks along and eats grass, converting it to good edible beef. What could be better than that? I will never understand people who buy countless thousands of dollars worth of labor saving machinery, tear up good grass, plant it to some crop to be harvested by another piece of labor-saving machinery and hauled somewhere to be fed to a cow. These people often have so much labor-saving machinery that they have to work seven days a week to pay for the stuff!

There are other drawbacks to labor-saving machinery. A fella I know from near Reva, SD told me that for many years his wife fed the cow herd with an old open air M International. Two years ago they splurged and bought a new front wheel assist loader tractor with cab and heat. She had this outfit to use during the winter of '96 and '97. She really liked the outfit, but as Lynn said, "Gosh, she sure wasted a lot of hay."

179

Up Sims Creek

By: Rod Nelson

"SRVs" bring adventure and good folks together

Times are tough here at Sims. Now and then I seem to need a little break just to get my spirits up. It dawned on me the other day that I had never been to the Miles City Bucking Horse Sale. Only those people who are severely socially deprived have never been to Miles City for the Bucking Horse Sale.

I felt somewhat guilty taking off with so much work to be done here around Sims, so I decided to ask my friend Bronc for advice. The only time Bronc was ever known to sweat was once when his air conditioner failed. "Bronc," I asked, "What do you think I should do this weekend, go to the Buckin Horse Sale or stay home and work?" "Stay home and work," Bronc said smugly. I knew I was in desperate need of a second opinion! Wasn't long 'til Jack walked in and gave me the advice I needed. "Go for it," Jack said.

As soon as I left the yard, the missus and the kids thought they should take a trip as well. Commandeering my '87 D250, they headed out for Bismarck. After eating at a Bismarck restaurant, they attempted to start my Dodge. Not realizing everything is backwards in a Dodge, my daughter jammed the key in the ignition the wrong way and it stuck tightly. The missus, utilizing mechanical techniques learned from me, quickly twisted it off, leaving the Dodge disabled.

I guess it serves them right for not packing a lunch on a major trip.

It was not a big problem. Due to the type of vehicles I drive, I am on a first-name basis with various mechanics, strategically placed throughout the Great Plains. When you have a problem in the "Bis-Man" area you call Ron Blank of Twin City Auto.

I first met Ron years ago. I was driving my car in lovely downtown Mandan when a front wheel fell off. Luckily it skidded right up to a convenience store so we could all enjoy sodas while we pondered our situation. I was sitting on the hood polishing

"SRVs" bring adventure and good folks together

off a Dr. Pepper when a pulchritudinous young lady driving by, stopped and said, "Mind if I take a look." "Go right ahead," I said.

She crawled under the car, looked it over, backed out and said. "My dad could fix that."

Her dad has been fixing stuff for me ever since.

Ron will work on most anything, but he seems to know a lot about SRV's. (Short Range Vehicles.) Many of his customers appear to be in the same income level as I am. Ron's shop is kind of a "Cowboys and Indians" place. I always like hanging around Ron's shop. There are often a few Sioux Indians around the place. I always enjoy visiting with Indians. It is a well known fact that Sioux Indians speak the best English in the German-Russian Triangle.

Anyway, when the missus needed help, Ron was soon there to lend a hand. Typically, Ron was ready to go the extra mile and offered to take my family back to Sims, a 45-mile trip.

Despite the protests of the missus, Ron soon had them loaded in a new SRV of his own and was heading west. "I am always happy to help out Rod," Ron said. "I have made a living for years on Rod's bad luck!" Things went well for awhile 'til Ron's vehicle started losing power and began belching clouds of smoke.

They had barely rolled to a stop when a fella I know from New Salem stopped and offered them a lift. Although he couldn't have recognized the vehicle, he no doubt sensed it contained members of the Nelson family.

Within minutes, Ron, the missus and the kids were once again on the way to Sims. It sure pays to know lots of good people.

It was a good weekend. We all had a chance to broaden our horizons, make new friends, and celebrate the Syttende Mai!

Up Sims Creek

By: Rod Nelson

Early TV didn't need a remote control - there was only one channel

Well, I guess it is summertime again at Sims. It is fairly warm, usually windy, and miserably dry. Freshly planted flowers, trees, and shrubs have that typical blow-torched look, so common here at Sims.

I was describing our rainfall to my friend Duane and he commented, "Kinda like stripping a dry cow huh?" I think my friend Rita maybe hit it on the head when she said, "It won't rain when we want it to rain, it will rain when we deserve it!" Could be dry for a spell at that rate. I suppose that could be true for those who get too much rainfall as well.

We are pretty much into the summer routine. Missed the big Seinfeld finale. Never did see too much of the Seinfeld show through the years, but did catch a show now and then. I guess missing the final episode isn't too traumatic for us. TV is kind of like sunburn, woodticks, frostbite, flu, and hogbutchering. It is a seasonal thing. Right now, TV is out of season.

I can't imagine people wasting time watching TV in the summer. TV watching is so non-productive compared to outdoor activities like watching grasshoppers dying of thirst, or observing carp churning up dust in the Sims Creek.

I guess my observations on TV should be worth something. I do remember when TV first hit rural North Dakota. TV at that time was really something. TV at that time was a little easier because there was no need for remote controls then. We only had one channel! TV was so unique, we watched Liberace twice a week just because there was nothing else to see.

I used to think it strange that Dad didn't know the names of TV programs or actors. He would sit in the living room watching TV with the rest of us, but he always had a book, paper, or magazine in his hand and the reading material always had top priority. I don't think Dad liked or disliked TV, he just seemed to tolerate it, at least in the wintertime.

Early TV didn't need a remote control - there was only one channel

We had a strange TV when I was a kid. Like most TV sets of the time, it took a lot of adjusting. There were adjustment knobs all over the back side. No color adjustment to worry about, but there were contrast controls, vertical and horizontal controls, etc. There was usually one person in every family who was somewhat handy with the adjustments on the family TV.

Our TV was strange because it seemed every year around the first of April the TV would go on the blink. No amount of tuning or adjusting would make the thing work. Dad would finally say, "Take that darn thing out into the porch, it doesn't work anyway. No use to have it sitting here in the way."

It didn't take long to forget about TV. There are countless things to do when you are not distracted by television. No one in our family missed the TV very much.

Late in the fall when the evenings started to get pretty long, someone would get the bright idea of dragging the TV back into the house and plugging it in. Lo and behold, the TV would work! And it would keep on working until at least around the first of April. I remember well that the TV acted just like that for several years.

I have thought about that TV many times. I never did ask Dad about it and he never volunteered any information about sabotaging the machine so I don't know if he did or not. I do know that TV is not a necessary part of anyone's summer activities.

Whenever I hear someone complain that their children won't do anything but watch TV, I know it is not the kids with the problem, it is the parents that can't be without television. If the parents could wean themselves from the endless, mindless drivel of television, there is no reason why their televisions would have to work all the time, especially in the summertime!

Up Sims Creek

By: Rod Nelson

Race would've been easier if there'd been a 200 lb. and over class

Things are vastly improved here at Sims. It rained here steady for a week, bringing the total to just over an inch. It is amazing what a little rain can do for your mental health.

From time to time I have tried to do something for my physical health but each spring I seem to be in worse shape than the previous year. I know I should do something to physically improve myself but am unsure just what activity I should pursue. I have done a lot of horseback riding but that activity takes a lot more lard off the horses than it takes off of me. I knew I needed more physical activity. I have considered mountain climbing, scuba diving, sky diving, and golfing, but being an impecunious rancher from Sims, ND, I thought I better try something like jogging.

I did some reading on the subject and everything I read cautioned against starting any serious physically challenging activity unless first consulting a medical professional. I immediately drove to Dickinson and consulted Dr. Rowe (rhymes with Roe), DVM. "What do you think of me trying some running to get in top physical shape, Doc?" I asked. Doc not only recommended running, but said I probably should consider road racing. "You see Rod," Doc commented, "many people are merely content to be physically fit, you have the potential to be a true athlete." I was elated when Doc volunteered to coach and train me in my new endeavor.

I started out slowly, running and walking every morning for a few weeks until I was finally able to run a full three miles at a steady, reasonable pace. Coach Rowe had me pumped up for a 5K road race in Bismarck on June 13. At first I was apprehensive. I told Coach Rowe that I knew I wouldn't be able to run very fast yet, and thought I might be out of place at such an event. "Don't worry about that" Coach Rowe assured me, "There will be many people just like you there. Not only will there be an age class, there will be a special class for people over 200 pounds. The most important thing in your first race is to participate and finish. Each race after that will be a challenge to improve your time."

Race would've been easier if there'd been a 200 lb. and over class

Things went well until May 27, when, due to an equipment malfunction, I was severely thrown from a horse. X-rays indicated that a couple ribs in my back were not broken like I thought they were, but merely severely bent. For a couple of weeks I couldn't breath easily, cough, or work. Running was out of the question. Finally, just a day before the big race, I called Coach Rowe and told him I would try it but wasn't sure if I could stand the pain. "Not to worry," he said with a sly wink, "I am a doctor you know."

Coach Rowe picked me up at 6:00 a.m. on June 13. He did a lot to build my confidence on the way to the big race in Bismarck. I was somewhat concerned that my attire would look out of place and that I wouldn't fit in with all these experienced runners. It was gratifying to learn that these were really nice people, and not only were friendly, but supportive as well. One fella commented that he had never seen running shoes colored like mine. I admitted that I did my stretching exercises in the barn each morning and it could be something I picked up in the horse stalls.

Coach Rowe did a lot of stretching and running around before the race but in an effort to conserve energy I mostly leaned against the pickup. I was somewhat dismayed that there was no class for the over 200-pound crowd. A quick appraisal of the entrants revealed that if there was such a class, I was a dead cinch for either the gold or silver.

My back was still hurting, so I took Coach Rowe aside and asked him if he had anything for my back pain. Coach Rowe looked both ways, reached into his pocket and handed me a rawhide dog biscuit, and told me to chew on it if the pain got too bad.

At the starting gate, I hung back. Being naturally considerate, I thought I would let the other fat guy run ahead of me for awhile. He was pathetic. Quite a lot shorter than me, he had to at least equal if not exceed me in weight. His legs looked like a couple sacks of spuds.

Race would've been easier if there'd been a 200 lb. and over class

They fired the gun and we were off. I started slowly, so did the fat guy. He wasn't a pretty sight. He had a gait like someone who had spent most of his life hanging onto plow handles. The true pros like Coach Rowe were soon out of sight. It wasn't long until it was pretty much just me and the fat guy. I felt sorry for him and decided I wouldn't pass him until after the first mile marker.

It was warm and humid. I wasn't real comfortable, but I wasn't doing badly. It was pretty easy-going. Unlike my training course, there were no holes or cow turds to dodge, just plain smooth asphalt. I tried to think up things to say to the fat guy when I passed him.

At the first mile marker the fat guy had a 100-yard lead on me. I was half mad at him. I knew if he collapsed I would have to run all the way around him or worse yet, might feel compelled to stop and give him first aid. I felt I was running a smarter race, conserving my energy for a big sprint in the final mile.

The fat guy was no longer in sight at the two mile marker. I smirked, assuming that he was out in the woods somewhere, puking!

Coach Rowe jogged back and met me about a half mile or so from the finish line and talked me through the rest of the race. You should have heard the cheers as I crossed the finish line! It was great! I do kind of wish the fat guy hadn't been sitting there near the finish line relaxing and sipping a Gatorade!

Coach Rowe took first place in the 40-49-year-old division with a time of 19:20. I was a little slower with a time of 29:40. Many people were impressed with my first race and I could tell Coach Rowe was proud of me.

I noticed several women acting somewhat light-headed around me so I asked Coach if that is the effect we athletes have on women. "Absolutely," he said, "of course it could have something to do with the ammonia smell coming off your shoes!"

Up Sims Creek

By: Rod Nelson

National Anthem stirs patriotism no matter how it's presented

Well, the 4th is upon us once again. I hardly know what other people do on July 4th. There are just a very few times in my life when I didn't spend July 4th at a rodeo, many times at several rodeos.

I probably have heard the "Star Spangled Banner" more times at rodeos than at any other event. I have heard the tune countless times, played on scratchy, bad, old phonographs, sung live by enthusiastic, but little talented people, and often sung by very good singers. Regardless of how the tune is played or sung, it seems to stir the listener with some emotion.

I heard an interesting rendition of the "Star Spangled Banner" at a Wyoming rodeo a couple years ago. The singer, a very talented young man, was really getting into the song when a bronc who was not too impressed, blew up in the chutes just below the crows nest. The young fella became completely flustered, forgot the words to the song and somehow switched over to "America the Beautiful." It was probably the most humorous interpretation I have ever heard of the patriotic and emotional National Anthem.

Once during the Bicentennial, I was attending a ten-performance rodeo in Iowa. A special performer at the rodeo was Pat Boone, who sang not only the National Anthem, but a stirring medley of patriotic songs like "Anchors Aweigh," "Off We Go," and the "Marine's Hymn." I can remember how great he sounded in the first couple performances.

Pat was evidently happy with his routine as he didn't change a thing for the entire ten performances. By the last day I could have cheerfully watched Pat stand before a firing squad!

The most chilling thing I have ever witnessed during the National Anthem was once

National Anthem stirs patriotism no matter how it's presented

many years ago in Cheyenne. Two beautiful, young ladies who were flying the colors wide open accidentally crashed their horses head on as they met in front of the bucking chutes. It was the worst wreck I have ever seen at a rodeo. Both horses were killed and both girls injured!

It always seems to stir patriotism when the "Star Spangled Banner" is heard outside and Old Glory is cracking in a stiff breeze.

Strangely enough though, the most patriotic emotion I have ever felt at a rodeo was not even in the United States.

I will never forget that day! I was at a little rodeo in Gainsborough, Saskatchewan. It was a hot, miserable, dusty day in July of 1969. Neither my traveling partners nor I were having much luck. None of the horses we had drawn had bucked enough to get us into the money.

We were standing around like poor, hapless, eleemosynary waifs when halfway through the performance the announcer suddenly stopped the rodeo and exclaimed, "LADIES AND GENTLEMEN, THE AMERICANS HAVE JUST LANDED ON THE MOON!"

I believe every Canadian at the rodeo ran to their cars, blew their horns and cheered and applauded wildly! It was a long time before the cheering stopped. It was a long time before the goosebumps faded, too!

Up Sims Creek

By: Rod Nelson

Ol' dad's still got it when it comes to bottle calves!

We have been reliving old times here at Sims lately. I have a son who is an aspiring roper and he was lamenting the fact that it is hard to practice calf roping when he has no calves. I suggested he purchase some day-old calves at the local auction barn.

He pestered me for a couple weeks and last week we made a trip to Mandan for the sale. We looked the calves over before the sale began and I gave him lots of valuable information about buying calves. "You can't go wrong buying quality, Son," I told him. "And just buy vigorous, healthy calves so they will be easy to feed and take care of and you might just as well buy all black bull calves so you will have a nice bunch when you want to sell them." I made him do all of the bidding himself, but sat close by in case he needed me.

He paid too much for most of them, but he was taking my advice and buying only nice, healthy bull calves. I couldn't understand it when he passed up a nice heifer calf that was selling a little too cheap and finally drilled him in the ribs when a couple light tan calves came in the ring. "I thought I was supposed to buy only black calves" he said. "Never pass up a bargain," I told him. I had to wake him up a little later when a couple white calves came in the ring with several others. They were selling "choice" and he was the successful bidder on a dandy white calf. The auctioneer asked if he would like to take more calves for the same money, so he turned and asked me what he should do. "It's your money, Son, pick whatever you want." He picked out a small black bull calf. "What did you pick that scrub for!" I asked. "Good grief! He was the poorest calf in the bunch!"

He was an ambitious bidder and with my continuing advice and support, he soon had purchased eight calves, one white, one gray, two light brown, one red, and three black calves. He made it to the office and settled up for the calves and we soon had them loaded, and we headed for the feed store. He let out a heavy sigh when he

Ol' dad's still got it when it comes to bottle calves!

wrote a check for the milk replacer. I also had him purchase some pails for feeding the calves. "Just buy plain pails, Son, nipple pails are just an unnecessary expense. You can teach them to drink like I used to when I was a kid." I then gave him the best advice he got from me all day. "You know, Son, you may be smart to take your sister on as a partner in this project. She can pay for half the feed and help you feed them."

His sister didn't hesitate to get in on the project and soon paid up her half of the expenses. She loved the calves, especially the little anemic calf her brother had picked on his own. She called him Brady.

Being a good father I willingly went out with the kids to mix the milk replacer and feed the calves the first time. I showed the kids exactly how to proceed. "Just back the calf in a corner, straddle him, hold the pail in your left hand, and put your fingers from your right hand in his mouth. When he sucks your fingers good, gently lower his head into the milk. He will soon learn to drink on his own. Remember, patience is the key."

I picked the biggest calf to demonstrate on. I suppose it had been at least thirty years since I had trained a pail calf to drink and had forgotten just how sharp the teeth on a calf can be. The big calf was a quick learner, however, and drank pretty well. The sharp teeth on my fingers actually bothered me less than the other calves sucking on my ears as I bent to my task. I suggested we separate the calves and feed them one at a time.

The feeding actually went quite well, other than occasional screams of pain and some crying over spilled milk. My daughter hated the white calf. He was extremely aggressive and bunted her around the pen. He soon acquired the name "Hitler." One of the light brown calves was dimwitted and wouldn't suck very good. Brady was about the only one that drank on his own the first time.

Ol' dad's still got it when it comes to bottle calves!

It was nice to have a project where the kids could look to me for advice. With my help, by the third feeding only the gray calf and the brown calf were having problems drinking. I could have cheerfully killed that brown calf. You never saw anything so stupid! I tried everything from a nipple bottle, to pouring the milk over his head, to the drink or drown method, and nothing seemed to work. Luckily, the kids don't seem to have too much trouble with him!

Up Sims Creek

By: Rod Nelson

Mom could put on a feed on very short notice

Things have been busy here at Sims. Had a housefull of company over the weekend. Don't know how everyone got fed around here, but I doubt if anyone left here hungry. Seems like there is always plenty to eat around here, especially when company is expected.

Unexpected company used to get my mother upset. I think the only thing about unexpected company that bothered my mother was the fact that she worried that she wouldn't have a proper meal for the guests. Scandinavian women are not about to let anyone off the place without properly feeding them. The company could be anyone from friends stopping by to visit, salesmen, preachers, relatives, or people with car trouble. It didn't matter, they were invited for a meal.

Mom hated to be surprised with company when she didn't have enough food for a good meal. In such cases Mom had to rely on "fast food."

I can still see the look on Mom's face when someone would drive in the yard pretty close to dinnertime. "Darn," Mom would say, "I don't have a blame thing for dinner."

Mom's panic would soon fade away and she would get serious. Mom could do more things at one time than anyone I have ever seen. Mom could boil water, sweep floors, knead bread dough and swat flies at the same time

As soon as the water was heated up good, Mom would sneak out of the house taking care that the "company" wouldn't see her. She would vault the yard fence and sprint for the barn, making Jackie Joyner-Kersee look like a foundered plow horse.

Any chicken that didn't have a hundred-yard lead never had a chance outrunning Mom if she had unexpected company. Seconds later at the chopping block, Mom's axe would flash and the hapless chicken's day was ruined!

Mom could put on a feed on very short notice

The poor bird barely had time to do the "dead chicken" thing before Mom was back in the basement scalding it in hot water. Next, a wad of newspaper was set on fire in the furnace and the singeing was soon done.

I can't remember Mom ever being squeamish about gutting a chicken and that chore was done quicker than most people can pick their nose. A heavy butcher knife and a real heavy duty scissors were used to cut the chicken up in the proper parts.

While the chicken was browning, Mom would dive out into the garden, grab a few fresh vegetables, cut a few gladiolas, and dig a few new potatoes before she low-crawled back to the house.

When Dad and the company finally walked up to the house, Mom would have a fresh dress on, the table set, and a "fast food" meal of chicken almost ready to eat.

A typical remark from Mom at this time would be something like, "Oh, I wish I had known you were coming, I could have had something decent to eat."

I suppose modern fast food is just a little quicker than Mom's but the quality is nowhere near the same.

If the "Colonel" had ever eaten Mom's chicken, he darn sure wouldn't have bragged about his recipe!

Up Sims Creek

By: Rod Nelson

Want to see a family movie? Take the weatherman's advice

In an effort to cut expenses here at Sims, I decided I could save on repairs if we just went to the show Saturday night, rather than stay in the field wearing out machinery.

It is always a struggle to pick out a show we can all see, as the missus is strict about what shows are suitable for family viewing. For instance, she doesn't think I should be seeing any PG-13 shows. She seems to be very concerned about the adult content of the modern shows. My protests that I am already 49 years old fall on deaf ears.

The language used in modern shows is of a big concern to her. I have to agree with her on that point. I am hardly a prude. I spent one winter as a roughneck, working on oil drilling rigs in North Dakota and Wyoming, I spent some time working on construction in the power plants, I have sorted tens of thousands of cattle, started hundreds of colts, driven a Dodge pickup, watched men load hogs, baled barley straw, and come home late when the missus was really hot. I know something about strong language! I do not, however, need to pay good money to hear a lot of trashy language in a movie!

We held a family council and checked the movies that are currently showing in Bismarck. I chaired the meeting. Each family member was allowed to vote for the movie of their choice. I don't know what they voted for. I didn't pay much attention. When everyone had finished I said, "We are going to see 'The Mask of Zorro.'" I don't know if I had a flashback to my youth, or just liked the preview of the show I had seen earlier.

The missus bristled right up and said. "That show is a PG-13." "No problem," I said, "I heard Jerry Bartz, the weatherman, talking about the show on the radio the other day and he said the show was entertaining and a decent family show." "What does Jerry Bartz know about movies," the missus wanted to know. "Well," I said, "He is a weatherman, the law of averages would tell us he is bound to predict

Want to see a family movie? Take the weatherman's advice

something accurately one of these days."

I drove the family to Bismarck, the missus bought some popcorn and pop. Thirty seconds into the show I was grinning broadly. Zorro was grand! Zorro was a good guy. There were bad guys in the show, but Zorro was smarter and tougher. Zorro rode a black stallion, did some fancy riding, fought a lot of bad guys, met a lovely maiden, helped a lot of poor people, and won the maiden's heart.

Zorro made me cheer, Zorro made me laugh, Zorro made me feel good! It was a little hard on the missus cause every time Zorro would swing his sword, instinctively I'd duck and scatter some of the missus' popcorn. I was a little tired by the end of the movie, but walked out of there stepping high!

You would hear rougher language at a Lutheran Ladies' Aid meeting than at that movie. There was some violence, but nothing worse than one can see when Blue Heelers lay down in rural women's flower beds.

We all loved the show. We talked about it all the way home. We talked about it the next morning at breakfast.

I finally asked the family in what ways they thought Zorro and I were alike. My daughter sat in silence, the missus said something about all the work she had to do and finally my son said, "Did he wear the mask and hat to cover up a bald spot?"

I thought I would just show them. I walked outside, jumped the yard fence, and picked up a cattle sorting stick. It made a suitable substitute for a sword. I held it out in front of me, put one hand behind my back and walked up to my Red Heeler dog and said "En Garde, Reuben." Strangely enough, no one seemed impressed!

Up Sims Creek

By: Rod Nelson

As the saying goes, "Anything beats working for wages"

Things are getting back to normal here at Sims. My yearly job with Bent Nail Construction is over and I can get back to doing the stuff I am supposed to be doing.

It seems strange in a way that I take this summer job each year. After all, the main reason I live here at Sims is to avoid the monotony of regular work; although working for Bent Nail Construction is not really regular work.

I'll admit that I have an aversion to regular, wage-paying jobs, and have been fortunate through most of my life to avoid them except for short periods as a roughneck, laborer, heavy equipment operator, truck driver, farm hand, and high school teacher.

I often have thought of a time when I stopped in to visit my old friend, Bud.

I met Bud and Billy out on the road. They were heading out to get a load of hay.

"We'll be in soon," Bud said. "Go down to the house and wait for us."

I didn't expect to see Billy working with Bud. I didn't realize he had retired from his regular job. Billy was obviously having a good time helping Bud haul hay. It was with more than a little pride, Billy told me later at the house, that he wasn't working for wages at Bud's ranch – some beef now and then or whatever.

Billy made it clear he was more than happy with whatever arrangement they had. The main thing I remember was a statement Billy made to me.

"I haven't worked for wages since I retired. Do you remember the show called the 'Rounders' with Glen Ford and Henry Fonda? They were all busted up and broke trying to break horses for a living, but one of them said, 'This still beats wages,

As the saying goes, "Anything beats working for wages"

anything beats wages.' They were right," Billy said. "Anything beats wages."

That is the best thing about working for Bent Nail Construction. You don't have to worry about wages! In fact, every non-paid worker on the crew does better than our boss, Keith. At least we don't have any expenses.

Keith came to visit relatives in Almont a few years ago. One day Keith spied an old building on Almont's main street. Formerly the "Holritz Store," the old two story building looked to most people like a future demolition project. Its only inhabitants were bats, cats, and pigeons. It drew Keith like a magnet.

"Hey! This building shows promise. This is restorable! This is a great old building! I could fix this up in my spare time!"

It sounded like a logical idea for someone who lived 1800 miles away in Alabama!

I tried to help Keith out by dropping every negative comment I could think of about such a project.

Keith was persistent. Within a year he had managed to swing a deal and was the owner of the old store.

As regular as mosquitoes in June, pheasant hunters in October or politicians at the annual Almont lutefisk supper, Keith Pitman returns each summer to spend his two-week vacation working on the old Holritz Store in Almont.

My family and I have managed to get minor positions on Keith's crew. We all managed to pass the entry requirements –which is to possess a warm body.

Keith's eclectic crew seems to grow each year. This year he showed up with Ron, a semi-retired dentist from an affluent suburb of Birmingham. A kindly fellow with a

As the saying goes, "Anything beats working for wages"

serene demeanor, he seemed somewhat perplexed as to why he was here, but obviously enjoys being part of the crew.

Jeff, Keith's nephew, 18 years old, fresh out of high school in Minnesota, came this year as an apprentice. He wasn't sure why he was here, perhaps he wanted to observe for himself if insanity runs in his family.

Jan, Keith's brother, a sure nuff tough ex-cop and detective from Minneapolis, came here a couple of years ago, I think to humor his brother. Each year I can see him get swept further and further into the project.

Sig, of Almont, almost 89 years old, just about the same age as the Holritz Store, still outworks most of Keith's crew.

When my son and I get essential chores out of the way, we head to Almont to join the crew.

No one seriously questions Keith about what he intends to do with the building. I don't think Keith really knows. Keith, like Alex Haley, probably is thinking about his roots.

Maybe he thinks about his Grandmother who no doubt shopped in the store during her childhood in Almont. A Minnesota native, he obviously feels some kinship to the little spot on the prairie where his grandparents, also from Minnesota, once lived.

It will be a big project to fix up the old store. One sees comparisons with Keith's project and the Crazy Horse Monument in the Black Hills – started in the late 1940s and still a long way from completion.

My contribution to the project is mostly as a common laborer. But, no matter if I am shoveling junk and bird feculence out of the upstairs or straddling the roof peak,

As the saying goes, "Anything beats working for wages"

so sharp it could split a raindrop, removing old shingles, it feels good to be part of the crew.

I have never had a bad boss, but Keith is one of the really good ones. He appreciates whatever we have to contribute. Keith would be just as happy helping me on some project. He is one of those guys that would make a darn good neighbor!

I like working for Keith. Whatever little time I contribute is probably time well spent. I often think of Mom quoting my grandmother, "You never lose what you give away."

Besides, it sure beats working for wages!

Up Sims Creek

By: Rod Nelson

Pie is one dessert that should never be passed up!

When times get really tough here at Sims I've found that a good piece of pie will darn sure improve your spirits. I have been around good pie-makers all my life. I wouldn't dare list any of the good pie-makers I have known as I would hate to arouse the wrath of those I may unknowingly omit.

I am not one who needs a dessert to top off a meal. I am not one who ever passes up a dessert either, but I really don't care that much about desserts. Very few desserts in my opinion can top a good beef dinner. Pie, though, now pie, is something one shouldn't pass up.

Everyone has their favorites, but my prairie heritage causes me to lean heavily toward Juneberry as my personal favorite. Chocolate is probably the only popular kind of pie that I really don't care much for.

Etiquette demands that the pie-maker should be complimented. There are times when that can be difficult. My old friend Ray started baking pies in his 70s after his wife passed away. Green tomato pie was Ray's specialty. I never had green tomato pie any other place but Rays, but eating it was a real challenge.

Ray would insist I come in for pie, serve me a generous piece and watch me carefully as I ate it. It was a difficult job. If you ate it too slowly Ray would be disheartened. If you ate it too fast and bragged on it too much, Ray would give you another piece! Regardless of whether or not I enjoyed the pie itself, it was always good to share that ritual with my friend Ray.

Pie is a special treat. Pie is something you can eat for pleasure when you are really not hungry.

The sad thing about pie is the fact that it is dangerous to order pie in a restaurant! Almost every cafe has a sign reading "Delicious Home-Baked Pies." They should be

Pie is one dessert that should never be passed up!

sued for false advertising. Although a good piece of pie can often be found, there is a lot of pie out there that would give a Blue Heeler stomach cramps!

The missus and I stopped at a prominent Bismarck restaurant one evening. The missus ordered lemon meringue. She made me taste the meringue. It was very similar to Styrofoam browned with a blowtorch.

I had blueberry. The filling was bad enough, but the crust! One could find better crust on a bachelor's coffee cup! It was bad beyond description! I was half mad at my mother for teaching me to clean up my plate. I'd have killed for a piece of Ray's green tomato pie about then, just to kill the taste in my mouth.

The waitress came by and said, "Did you enjoy your pie?"

"Very good. Great!" the missus and I said in unison. My conscience jerked severely!

I have made a resolution to avoid ordering pie anymore in cafes, unless I am familiar with the place.

Luckily I can still get a good piece of pie in the Sims area. If you come to Almont on a Wednesday and only Wednesday, you can enjoy a good piece of homemade pie that my friend Marion bakes. She serves it at Pat and Penny's floral. It isn't hard to find. Just head down main street in Almont and go into a building with several cars in front. You will either be at the flower shop or the bar. It is worth the trip.

The price? It is whatever you feel like contributing. In my opinion, going to Almont and eating Marion's pies is time and money well spent!

Up Sims Creek

By: Rod Nelson

Kaycee, WY is a "good time had by all" kind of place

Things have picked up here in drought-stricken Sims. We've had over 5 inches of rain since Mid-August. This country looks like it had a dandy facelift.

I had the good fortune to go back to Kaycee, WY again this year for the Deke Latham Memorial Rodeo on September 12-13. This is the third year in a row I have been there. The missus has a hard time understanding why I wanted to drive that far and stay so long, just to see a rodeo.

I have to admit that I really look forward to attending this annual event. I already seem to know enough people in Kaycee that going to the rodeo is like attending a reunion.

It seems like there is a different attitude in Kaycee. People are a lot more casual there. They don't seem to sweat the small stuff. When they trail the bucking horses down Main Street and they break out and run through someone's yard, no one seems to get too excited. The parade doesn't get much bigger and there isn't much for fancy floats, but more people line the street to watch the parade every year.

I had the good fortune to be one of the entertainers at the annual Hole in the Wall Poetry Ball. It is nice to entertain a crowd that needs no explanation for any of my stories of rural life.

Ross Buckingham attended the event and gave me heck the next day for causing him to have to chain up all four wheels on his pickup when he was caught in a downpour on the way home to his mountain ranch. Mrs. Buckingham explained there are a lot of bad drop-offs along the dirt road and every time they slide down to the low spots, she prays and Ross cusses. She takes the credit for the safe trip home.

This year I met Harold Jarrard. I believe he is 79 years old. Harold is still an active pickup man in Wyoming rodeos. He has the trim look of a 20-year-old with another 60 years of toughness thrown in. Smoking cigarettes is still one of the safer

Kaycee, WY is a "good time had by all" kind of place

things that Harold does on a daily basis.

It rained in Kaycee on Sunday. It was miserable to rodeo in the rain, but everyone agreed it was grand to see such a wonderful rain. There were a lot of nice mud puddles around the arena and grandstand. Little kids with new cowboy boots were having a fine time running through the puddles. They have young mothers wise enough to let them do it.

Like usual, the horses bucked pretty good, despite the mud. There weren't any sensational rides this year, but lots of good solid rides. It was a good rodeo.

Like anywhere stockmen live, good stories abound! I heard lots of good ones about cattle, horses, rattlesnakes, sheepshearers and Scotchmen.

I know Kaycee can't be as good as I think it is. No doubt Kaycee has its share of village idiots, land hogs, insufferable bores or people who think body odor alone is enough to contribute to society. All I know is that these people don't seem to stand out during the rodeo. Not everyone would think three days of visiting in Kaycee would be so fun, but it was grand to me.

Some day next January when it is 20 below I'll probably be out, half frozen to the seat of my open air Oliver, pushing snow, when all of a sudden I'll remember one of Ross Buckingham's stories. The missus will be looking out the window wondering why I am laughing out loud. That is why I love to go to Kaycee!

Up Sims Creek

By: Rod Nelson

The family that gardens together . . . eats tomatoes forever

Things are moving slow here at Sims. There's lots of work left to do. About the only thing I have finished this fall is gardening. Frost put a humane end to that.

I have had a hard time getting my family enthused about gardening. I have always believed that rural people should have a garden, so I held a family meeting one day and decreed that we would all have a garden this year. The old garden that was too much for the missus to handle alone would be divided into four equal parts and each of us would have our own garden and compete to see who could do the best job. I gave a spirited lecture on benefits of eating wholesome, organically grown vegetables. I also decided that each of us could decide what we would like to plant. I would keep a journal so we would have a permanent record of the gardening season.

May 22: The missus asked if she could hire someone to till the garden. I tore the fence down and did a beautiful tillage job with the tractor and disc. Rebuilt the fence. Put an extra barb wire on this year. Found a corral panel to use as a gate. Took the family to town to buy seed. As the leader and needing to set an example I purchase a diverse selection: Carrots, peas, beans, onions, radishes and for an extra touch I buy marigolds for a border and 18 gladiola bulbs for a late summer surprise bouquet.

May 28: The missus set out tomato and cucumber plants and planted beets. She chastised me for not planting anything yet. I tell her it is too early. I notice that my daughter hasn't planted anything either. I give her a lecture on responsibility. She still refuses to plant anything.

June 2: Frost! All the missus' plants are dead. I tell her, "I told you so."

June 4: I happen to be in Dickinson and in a spirit of generosity, purchase some tomato plants I find on sale for the missus. The missus isn't impressed, but I tell her the little plants are the best ones.

June 5: I'm sick and tired of everyone telling me that my marigolds are almost dead

The family that gardens together . . . eats tomatoes forever

so I head to the garden to plant. Cleverly, I dig a long trench for the marigolds so I can water them easily. I plant all my seeds while I am out there. Hate to brag, but I did do a beautiful job. Told the missus she better get her tomatoes planted. Got my son to plant his garden. He goes right to work, seeds watermelon, corn and potatoes. My daughter still refuses to get her part planted.

June 6: Catch the missus watering her garden with water from the rural water pipeline. I tell her it costs money and our high sodium well water would work just as well. Convince my daughter she has to get her garden planted. She spends a total of five minutes out there. Plants a few hills of squash and pumpkins. I chastise her for the ugly garden she will have. "All that bare ground will look bad," I tell her.

June 21: Check the garden. Everyone's seeds are up but mine. My marigolds are gamely hanging in there, but I am getting tired of digging them out of the mud each time I flood the trench.

June 22: The missus leaves early for the day. I gather all the hoses and connect them to the rural water spigot on the house. Soak my garden down really good. Have hoses put away before the missus gets home.

June 23: Discover that some idiot has left the gate open to the garden. Eight horses have been in there. They sure sunk deep in the mud in my section. Looks like a moonscape.

June 30: Hurrah! Beans are up, carrots are up, radishes and onions look great where the horses didn't step. Only two peas have come up. No sign of the glads.

July 14: Decide to weed the garden before I can't find the rows. Still only two peas up, decide to summerfallow that part with my hoe. Find only three gladiolas. Call my mother for advice. "You planted them right side up, didn't you?" she said. Radishes look so good I can't bring myself to dig them up.

The family that gardens together . . . eats tomatoes forever

July 30: Grasshoppers hit! Glads gone, half the carrots gone, onion tops completely gone. Grab a hoe and convert glad patch to summerfallow. While I am at it, I put the marigolds out of their misery. Weeded the beans, grasshoppers had half of the row consumed, but found nice beans growing on the other half. Found a bag of fly dust for cattle, and dust my carrots and beans heavily. Read the directions after I was done and learned I had applied at least 100 times the recommended rate.

Aug. 1: Checked the garden. Mine looks like a hazardous waste dump. Grasshoppers moved into potatoes and corn. Evidently they don't eat tomato plants and pumpkins. The daughter's garden is a solid mat of leaves. The missus' tomato plants look like haystacks.

Aug. 2: Proudly pick a capful of nice green beans and ask the missus to cook them for supper. No one will eat them but me. Guess they haven't developed a taste for Methoxychlor.

Aug. 20: Noticed that late rains have washed the beans and carrots off so nicely that the grasshoppers have finished them off. Converted the rest of my garden to summerfallow. Didn't really need my vegetables any more with all the tomatoes we are eating.

Oct. 1: Very hard frost at Sims. All leaves are wilted to nothing. Sure is a mess with all the tomatoes going to waste. Will have to get a truck in there to haul all those pumpkins and squash. My garden looks great! Very neatly tilled.

Conclusion: Gardening project a big success. I think the family has learned so much from it, they won't even need my input next year!

Up Sims Creek

By: Rod Nelson

Good luck, John Glenn – we'll leave the light on for you!

The signs point to Fall here at Sims. Leaves are gone, there is often frost on the windshield, and if I don't strain my coffee through my teeth, I am bound to swallow a few boxelder bugs.

It is time to haul hay again. I am not among the weakhearted who haul hay in too early, besides, I am not done haying yet and I believe in first things first. I never did believe in hauling hay early. Fire is one of the few things that worries me. Early hay hauling, I feel, is just too dangerous. I always follow a simple rule to determine if I should be hauling hay. I never, never haul hay until all the twine has rotted off my round bales. If the bales still have twine, you are either hauling too early, it is too dry, or it is just plain too easy. Who wishes to go through life without challenges?

Another sign of Fall is this darn political advertising. The political ads this year are about as refreshing as a week-old lutefisk sandwich! I really don't think they do much to truly educate the voter. I am almost glad the missus won't let me watch much TV. The ads are nearly as disgusting as the prime time TV shows!

The only politician in the news lately that really perks up my interest is the Democrat Senator from Ohio, John Glenn. No doubt, there are people who don't know that John Glenn is a U.S. Senator. A lot of people don't realize that as a Marine Corps pilot, John Glenn flew something like 149 combat missions in WWII and in Korea. I didn't realize until recently that John Glenn was the first person to make a nonstop, transcontinental, supersonic flight from LA to New York in 1957, setting a new record. It is an ignorant person, however, who doesn't know that John Glenn was the first American to orbit the earth in space.

I remember it well. I was with my folks over at Henry Hoadley's place and watched the news that night on TV. He orbited the earth three times in four hours and 55 minutes. He traveled something like 81,000 miles that night. That has always

Good luck, John Glenn – we'll leave the light on for you!

amazed me until today, when it struck me that I have driven my 1987 3/4 ton Dodge pickup about the same distance in only seven years. Try topping that, John.

I think he will top it. John Glenn, at 41, was a gutsy old man on February 20, 1962. At 77, he is still a gutsy old man who plans to be on the space shuttle Discovery when it is scheduled to blast off on October 29.

I am used to older folks who are capable of doing things. I know octagenarians who still break their horses, calve their cows in early March, and farm with Molines. I am still impressed that John Glenn at 77 will attempt such a thing. I have heard that the odds of a fatal accident on such a trip could be as high as two percent. Not very good odds for me.

The whole world was watching on February 20, 1962. The citizens of Perth, Australia left all their lights on that night so he could see them. I hear that they plan to do that again. I wish we had more than one yardlight here at Sims.

I don't think that John Glenn is going up in space again to prove anything. No doubt he relishes the challenge. Perhaps he wishes to avoid one week of political advertising. I haven't met John Glenn. I don't know much about his political career. I somehow get the feeling, however, that he would make a good neighbor. He seems like the kind of guy who would help you pull your pump when it is 40 below. I think he would help you out when your stackmover is buried to the axles in gumbo. He probably would keep his fences up and spray his spurge.

I don't know if you get the "Farm and Ranch Guide," John, but if you do, my hat is off to you. Have a safe trip and if you happen to fly over Sims, lean out and look down. We'll leave the light on for you!

Up Sims Creek

By: Rod Nelson

School fundraisers create "who to sell to" dilemma

Times are tough here at Sims. Seems like every time I turn around there is someone trying to extract another dollar from me. Bills are bad enough, but there seems to be no end to the fundraising schemes.

My daughter came home the other day and informed me I had to buy a magazine subscription for a junior class fund-raiser. She had some kind of a quota and by the time the smoke cleared, she bought a subscription for herself, the missus ordered one and I had a subscription to a magazine I really didn't need or want very much.

My daughter was pretty happy with the sales she had made and soon had her quota filled. I wouldn't have thought much about it, but later I saw her signing several postcards and asked her what she was doing. "It's for the magazine sales," she said. "We are supposed to send five post cards to other people that encourage them to buy magazines from this company."

I looked at the postcards she had filled out and did a slow burn when I saw Grandmas and Grandpa, aunts and uncles. The very people who always support the kids.

I thought this was pretty underhanded salesmanship. My mind drifted back to my freshman year in FFA. Back in the days when fund-raisers were honest and straightforward.

I remember it well. Our FFA chapter at Towner was selling fire extinguishers to raise money. We were aware of farm safety and had been drilled to stress this when we went out and sold the fire extinguishers.

I teamed up with my neighbor Ricky. He was a couple of years older, but we were neighbors and it was logical that we work together. We picked a night to start selling and made a list of potential customers.

School fundraisers create "who to sell to" dilemma

We decided to take the easy pickings first and work our way up to the tougher ones as we learned the tricks of salesmanship. We decided to start early in the evening and hit several neighbors. Slim and Alice were to be our first customers and I think Shorty and Yvonne were next on the list, but anyway, we were at Slim's place early in the evening.

They seemed glad to have a couple neighbor lads over to visit and we were soon in the house having a good visit. We knew we should get right to the point, but it was early in the evening, Slim always had good stories to tell, and of course Alice was soon filling us up with lots of goodies.

I suppose we sat there a couple of hours before we realized we weren't cut out to be high pressure salesmen. We just couldn't seem to get around to talking fire extinguishers. I finally motioned to Ricky that he better quit talking and get to the point. Ricky's face turned a bit red, but he finally cleared his throat, looked Slim right in the eye, and said. "How are your bulls looking Slim?" Slim raised registered Herefords and we soon had a detailed report on the gain and condition of all of Slim's bulls.

Well aware of Ricky's pathetic salesmanship skills, I knew it would be up to me to get to the point ,but when I tried to ask if he would be interested in a fire extinguisher it came out more like "Have you seen any big bucks lately?" With Slim's love of hunting it would be a long time before we talked of anything else.

Midnight was close when Alice asked if we had school tomorrow. We admitted we did and slowly made our way to the door. I suppose we stood at Alice's kitchen with the door open until we dropped the temperature in the house twenty degrees. We were just walking out on the porch when Ricky finally blurted out, "Say Slim, our FFA chapter is selling fire extinguishers. Your wouldn't want one would you?" "Just

School fundraisers create "who to sell to" dilemma

thinking the other day that we should have a couple," Slim said. We were soon back at the kitchen table filling out the order forms. Ten minutes later we back in the car heading home, tickled that selling fire extinguishers was so easy.

Yes, that was good honest salesmanship, not like this underhanded magazine sales.

"You are not sending these postcards to these people," I told my daughter. "Well who do I send them to?" she wailed. "Our servants," I replied. "What servants?" she wanted to know. "Public servants," I said smugly. "Like who," she quizzed me. "Well, how about the North Dakota attorney general, the governor, and our senators?" She was warming up to my idea but wondered where we could find their addresses. "They are all right here in the phone book," I told her.

She soon had four cards filled out and asked who she should send the last one to. "Just what are you raising money for anyway?" I wondered. When she said it was for the junior class and was mostly needed for the prom I didn't hesitate. "Make this one to Bill Clinton, 1600 Pennsylvania Ave., Washington DC. All of a sudden I got to liking magazine sales better than peddling fire extinguishers!

Up Sims Creek

By: Rod Nelson

Road Rage only happens in urban areas – or does it?

Times are tough here at Sims. In times of high stress it is easy to over-react to things that shouldn't bother us so much. Take road rage for instance. Lots of people I visit with shake their heads in wonderment and disgust when they read or hear of another shooting on a Florida highway. "How can people stand to live there?" they ask in amazement. Actually "road rage" is commonplace all over rural America. Most of us don't refer to it as road rage however. Prairie Trail Rage or Township Road Rage is more like it.

Most of us experience Prairie Road Rage now and then. It usually happens when you are in a hurry. You jump in your vehicle, and head for your destination, comfortable with the knowledge that if everything holds together you can get where you are going just in the nick of time. Your vehicle is just getting up a head of steam when some knothead pulls out in front of you with a wide load of hay. His tractor is capable of doing twelve miles an hour but he is content to cruise along at about nine miles an hour. Back in your vehicle, you take a deep breath and tell yourself that he can't be going far. You pass up the first side road that you could use for an alternate route secure in the knowledge that he is going to turn off in just a minute. Ten minutes later you tell yourself it wouldn't be worth turning around and going back. Surely, even if he has a long way to go he will pull off and let you pass soon. Ten minutes more and you truly hate this person!

The truth of it is when a farmer or rancher gets old, usually around 35, once he gets his load on a road or trail he is oblivious to anything or anyone who might be following him. He may have had a series of unfortunate happenings like flat tires, blown hydraulic lines, broken spindles, or worse things and when he at last reaches a paradise like the road, he goes into some kind of a trance, dreaming about any one of a thousand pleasant things. Perhaps he fantasizes about making the interest payments, having rain next spring, or finding a girlfriend who can handle two pails of feed in each hand.

Road Rage only happens in urban areas – or does it?

At any rate, he is in fantasy world, as is the hapless soul who is following close behind. This individual dreams of capturing the tractor driver, binding him tightly and perhaps boiling him in oil or burning him at the stake.

I remember my Dad once when he got home from Rugby with a load of feed. It was mid-winter and the heater didn't work in his old truck. He was blue and trembling, mumbling something about following a stack of hay for something like seven miles. He was too frozen to stay mad. Just relieved that the ordeal was finally over.

Rural Road Rage is also common on better improved highways. The hay hauler probably has to make a left hand turn. He knows the probability of someone coming from behind is not great. He has probably crawled off his tractor several times to look back on an empty road and he is sick of it. He hopes he will meet a car just before his turn so he can quickly duck into the left side of the road. If there is no oncoming car he can either stop and get off or use the inch over method. This method gradually shoves any passing vehicle into the ditch if they aren't fortunate enough to stop in time. Most of us at some time have seen a semi driver at a truck stop, pulling hay off of his rear view mirrors and babbling incoherently about some farmer who tried to push him off the road with a load of hay.

Still, we don't hear of many cases of Road Rage that cause a shooting. Perhaps it is because us prairie dwellers are a more understanding, and patient people than others around the nation. Or perhaps it is because the wide loads of hay prevent us from getting a clear shot!

Up Sims Creek

By: Rod Nelson

Plan for winter by storing up a supply of good books

Things have really picked up here at Sims. This has been a season of mood swings. Early November snows made moods pretty low, but every warm, thawing day helps brighten spirits. I suppose it is a sign of old age, but the older I get the better I like the thought of a brown Christmas.

We have gone from knee deep snow to knee deep mud. I'll bet the overshoe people have enjoyed a lot of sales from the unseasonably muddy weather. It kind of puts a lot of ranchers in a dilemma for Christmas shopping, as they have already had to buy their wives new overshoes in November when usually they can wrap them up and surprise their wives on Christmas eve.

I don't know what I will get the missus this Christmas. I already splurged in October and bought her three loads of scoria for the driveway. She gets a thrill every time she can make it all the way in to the yard without getting stuck. What else could a woman want?

It looked pretty spooky early on in November when the big snow hit and I had lots of bales twelve miles from home. It really gave me a sinking feeling in the gut knowing I needed them badly to make the winter. The only consolation I had, was all the other people in the same shape. It was strangely comforting as I drove around the country with my family to see that lots of other people, also had bales to haul. It was easy to feel sorry for them and I would often comment, "Look, there is someone else who was caught with all the wet, fall weather and wasn't able to finish hauling bales."

A little break in the weather made it possible for me to really get rolling and in a few days I was able to finish all my bale hauling. I was trying to get it done before another snowstorm, but it turns out I was able to get them before the mud made it impossible.

It is fun to drive around the country now with the family. I will see a big field full of bales and comment. "Now there is a poor operator. What kind of a sap would let bales lay around until this time of the year?"

217

Plan for winter by storing up a supply of good books

We may not have "winter-like" weather now, but we darn sure are getting "winter-like" evenings. In other words, short days and long evenings. The days are getting so short that even I can put in a full days work!

Long evenings usually have me pawing through my bookcases looking for something to read, but that isn't my problem this year. I have come by lots of books from various sources this fall. I have a pile of books at least three feet deep next to my chair. I have everything from Will Rogers to physical fitness, from mountain men to occupied Norway, from cowboys to loggers, and from outhouse stories to tales of the Arctic.

That pile will be long gone by spring and I will have a new selection there.

One of the most interesting books in that pile is a regional book by the "50 Years in The Saddle" committee. This book, "50 Years In The Saddle, Volume IV" is hot off the press. With 565 pages and over 1200 pictures it is a lot of good reading. There is a lot of good stuff in this one. It has a tremendous amount of history recorded in easy to read, interesting stories and the photos are great. Just flipping through it as I write this, I see great photos of the old Sanish rodeo, glimpses of Casey Tibbs as a kid, lots of very good rodeo photos of North Dakota cowboys who are still around, and of course lots of stories of pioneering families from across the state. This book is not only readable, but well worth reading. It is worth having in your house if, for nothing else, than a reference book.

Postpaid, the books cost $76, so they aren't cheap, but they only printed 850 copies and there won't be any reorders, so it may be a good idea to order one soon. I am sure there are far more than 850 people who would really appreciate a copy for Christmas. They can be ordered from "50 Years in The Saddle," C/o Manfred Signalness, HC 3 Box 26B, Watford City, ND 58854. It will be money well-spent!

Up Sims Creek

By: Rod Nelson

"Merry Christmas from Sims and to all a good night"

Things have really picked up here at Sims. We have gone from an early November snowstorm to balmy mid-December weather. The missus' Uncle Sig Peterson claimed the grass kept growing through the snow. I do know for sure that he mowed the lawn at the Almont Lutheran Church on December 9th before he put up the Nativity scene.

Little children may deplore the lack of snow, but it doesn't bother old ranchers or cows. Despite the brown prairie, the signs of the Christmas season are upon us again. Christmas lights glow everywhere and the unmistakable feelings of Christmas are apparent.

One thing I really enjoy about the Christmas season is the mail we receive. There are always some Christmas cards in with the bills. There are a lot of nice people out there who keep sending us cards. I'll admit that we aren't quite so prompt at sending cards. Quite often there may be a year or two delay before we get them sent.

I especially enjoy getting all the nice photos that come at Christmas time. I will admit though, that I am less enthused about photos that only show the little children. It is not that I don't like children or cute photos of them but face it, kids are like puppies, they are all cute. I prefer to see photos of children with their parents so I have a better idea of who they belong to. I admire people who have guts enough to show the world how they look after the ravages of time.

Even my mother-in law was guilty of the "kids only" thing this year. Their lovely Christmas card contained pictures of all their grandchildren and the family dog, but no photos of themselves. I told her she would be a little more original if the card just had pictures of me and her daughters-in-law.

Form letters continue to be popular as they are so easy, but it still takes a lot of postage to mail them. I realized I could save some cash if I sent mine through this column so here goes.

"Merry Christmas from Sims and to all a good night"

Dear Friends and Readers,

On March 15th it will be 15 years since we moved from Towner to the Sims-Almont community. I am still adjusting to the change from the Mouse River to the Sims Creek, although it is now apparent we are pretty well established here. I realized we had been here awhile when I noticed one day that pretty much everything I have built since I moved here has either rotted down or fallen over.

It really has changed in the last 15 years. There wasn't a lot here when we came. I remember looking out the window and seeing nothing much but a lovely view of the old town site of Sims nestled along the Sims Creek between the rolling prairie hills. Now I see rows of rusting machinery along the fences, a sure sign of an established North Dakota farm or ranch. I have to admit I got a bit of a jump-start on my junk piles as most of the machinery I have acquired had already been in someones junk yard.

We came here 15 years ago with two babies. We now have two teenagers who, after grade school in Almont, attend high school in New Salem. They are good kids who despite my urging have not joined any gangs. There just arn't enough people in Sims to support one.

We still call ourselves ranchers, but like most young "Under 65-year-old" North Dakota farmers or ranchers, we do some other things to help support the cows.

The missus enjoys her part time job at Elm Crest Manor in New Salem. She likes working with the staff and residents at the rest home and is getting valuable experience for the time when I will be needing extra care.

I continue to enjoy my role as a small-time entertainer and public speaker. I have gotten to know a lot of great people through those experiences.

"Merry Christmas from Sims and to all a good night"

I also work as a brand inspector at the New Salem and Almont livestock sales. Mid-November marked the ten thousandth time I have been kicked since I started that career.

I still start quite a few colts for myself or for others. My horse training techniques have improved considerably in the last 15 years. I have to admit though, that colts still blow up and buck, fall down, or run through fences from time to time. Years ago I relied on my physical ability to ride them to a standstill or nimbly jump to safety. Now I merely shut my eyes, scream, and take the wreck! In an effort to improve my physical fitness I have been running from three to six miles a day for several months. My efforts must be apparent as someone told me they had asked my neighbor Joel how I was doing with my running. Joel solemnly agreed that it sure had been good for my appetite.

We have a hog in the freezer and a nice steer to butcher in a couple weeks. The cows look good, the propane tanks are full, and looks like the feed should last till green grass. My car only has 160,000 miles on it and the best thing is that every time I stop it and get out, I can find a friend.

A sincere thanks to those of you who toss a compliment my direction now and then. I am truly flattered when someone tells me they read my column.

So from all of us here at Sims, Merry Christmas and Happy New Year.

Up Sims Creek

By: Rod Nelson

None of us will ever forget New Year's Day in '59

If I were asked what holiday I remember most I would have to say New Years Day 1959.

We were expecting company at noon, but holiday or no holiday the cows have to be fed. Dad hitched up Dolly and Chub to the sleigh and we headed to the feed ring in the woods a mile or so northwest of the house along the Mouse River.

It was a typical North Dakota January day. It was cold, very cold and a lot of fresh Manitoba air was pouring across the meadow. I was nine years old and my brother Orrin was 13. It was an everyday trip for Dad, but for Orrin and me, it was fun to go along on the big hayrack.

After feeding the cows a few sacks of cake, Dad headed out again across the open meadow to get a load of hay. We were far enough away from the woods, so the wind was biting us pretty hard. Dad stood up in front, driving the team, but Orrin and I sat with our backs to the wind near the rear of the 10'x20' rack.

It happened so fast it is almost hard to explain it. Something like a mini hurricane or twister picked the hayrack up and flipped it like a pancake. Orrin and I were harmlessly pushed down in the snow and the rack missed us when it came down, but Dad landed right under it. I suppose Dad would have been killed if the team hadn't drug the rack off of him before they broke loose.

Dad was hurt, and hurt badly. He was in so much pain from injury to his leg and hip that he couldn't even crawl. Minor scalp wounds which covered his face with blood probably scared us more at the time.

Orrin, always practical, knew what he had to do. The team had stopped by a haystack close to us, and he ran to them, climbed up on old Dolly and flogged her for home.

None of us will ever forget New Year's Day in '59

There were no snowmobiles, or four wheel drives on our ranch in 1959. Orrin never wasted any time calling around for help, there was only one way to get Dad home. I don't know how he got old Prince saddled that fast, but it wasn't long before I could see him coming. Old Prince may not have been a race horse, but not many thoroughbreds could have beat him that day as he plunged through the deep snowbanks to the rescue. Behind him, crashing along wildly on a thirty-foot rope, was our main winter plaything, the hood off of a 1949 Kaiser car.

It took some doing to get Dad on the carhood, but with a lot of effort he finally made it. He sat, facing backwards, his hands gripping the sides of the hood. I can't remember where I sat, as Dad must have taken up most of the room, but I had a spot and a handhold somewhere. Orrin climbed up on Prince, dallied the rope on the saddle horn and we were off at a brisk trot.

The pain was so severe that even Dad thought he couldn't take it and he hollered to Orrin to slow down. It was a clear cut case of mis-communication. Orrin naturally thought he was being chastised for going too slow. He leaned over close to Prince's gray mane and lashed him every stride with the reins. Dad could no longer speak. His eyes had that glazed-over terror like a deer in a spotlight.

It must have been quite a scene. Imagine a "Howdy Doody-looking" kid in a tattered parka and four-buckle overshoes tied together with twine stuck in the stirrups of an old high-backed saddle. He was going so fast I swear he left a vapor trail, the carhood crashed along behind like a speed boat racing against whitecaps.

The straightaway was bad enough, but centrifugal force almost sent the hood airborne as we slid sideways on the corners. Chunks of snow thrown back from Princes hooves pelted the carhood like machine gun fire.

I will say one thing. The best trained paramedics in the country couldn't have gotten

None of us will ever forget New Year's Day in '59

Dad home so quickly. The carhood screeched to a stop on the bare ground in the yard and Mom ran out to help Dad into the house.

I don't recall how they got Dad to the hospital. He did spend a couple days there and he was laid up much of the winter. It was one of those things that aren't funny until the pain goes away. None of us will ever forget it. Dad laughed about it for the rest of his life. "Yup," he often said, "the wreck was bad enough, but that ride home, now that was something!"

Up Sims Creek

By: Rod Nelson

Outdone in the joke department by a 5-year-old!

Times are tough here at Sims. January makes things tough all over. It is the time of year when cows get skinny and people get fat.

Years ago, winter meant a lot of physical activity, and long hours outside burned up lots of calories. Now we move less and less in the winter and pay for it with tighter and tighter clothing.

Strangely enough, sports become more important in the winter. Spectator sports that is. For us North Dakotans, spectator sports mean mostly high school basketball or volleyball. The NBA lockout wasn't a life or death problem for most of us. High school sports, on the other hand become very important, especially if there are teenagers in your household.

I was attending a high school basketball game in New Salem last week. The Warriors from Fort Yates were playing the New Salem high school team. Although the Warriors were well in control, their fans were enthusiastically cheering every time their team made a point. It was fairly noisy in the gym. It is a time when us old duffers who can no longer see so well, can no longer hear so well either.

I was sitting there watching the game when my 5 or 6-year-old friend Garret came up to me and asked me if I would like to hear a joke. "Sure I would like to hear a joke," I told the youngster. Garret said, "What did the bug say when he hit the windshield?" I asked him what the bug said. "Wow, I don't have guts enough to try that again" the little joke teller replied.

I asked Garret if he would like to hear another joke? Of course he did, so I told him one I had heard recently. "What did the porcupine say when he backed into the cactus?" The answer being, "Is that you Mom?"

Garret seemed to like the joke well enough and he ran off. Later, as I walked back

Outdone in the joke department by a 5-year-old!

into the gym from a trip to the refreshment stand, I sat down to visit with Garret and his Mom. "Did you tell your Mom the joke I told you?" I asked Garret. When he told me he had forgotten to, I told him to go ahead and tell her. Garret had forgotten the joke by that time so I whispered the joke in his ear. Garret then slid close to his Mom and whispered it to her. Mom looked somewhat bewildered and turned to me and asked, "What did you tell him anyway?" I figured the little fella must have goofed up and had him come to me and I whispered the joke to him one more time. Once more he slid over to Mom and repeated the story. This time she swung around obviously agitated and said. "What are you try to teach my boy anyway?"

It took some pleading to get her to tell me what Garret had said, which turned out to be "What did the porcupine say when he backed into the cat piss?"

Somehow Garret's version turned out to be a lot funnier than mine!

Up Sims Creek

By: Rod Nelson

Cows huddle up against the cold – just like the smokers!

Times are tough here at Sims, but then, January makes times tough all over. Although this January has been better than many we have seen, the cold, windy, spells still tend to wear one down.

The cold weather is especially tough on all the critters that have to stand outside in the cold. On those especially frigid days, I can't help but feel sorry for my cows. They look miserable standing there with snow on their backs, trying to stay out of the wind.

I drove into Bismarck the other day and couldn't help but notice groups of cattle in similar situations all along the way. Of course one sees mostly females, the bulls being in a minority.

I was looking forward to the change of scenery when I reached the city but the view didn't change all that much. Wherever I drove I saw groups of people, mostly women, standing around, humped up, backs against the wind, taking a few desperate drags on a cigarette before ducking back inside to warmth and safety.

It struck me as I drove around, that even with cigarettes costing more and more all the time, smoking is a better value than ever. It used to be that cigarette smoking meant only bad breath, yellow teeth, smelly clothing, stained fingers, wrinkles, emphysema, heart disease and cancer. Nowadays you can add hypothermia and quick pneumonia to the list!

I feel for these people. I used to smoke a little myself. Back when I was smoking, smokers assumed they had rights. Almost everyone smoked. Your preacher most likely smoked, your barber smoked, your doctor smoked, and they smoked everywhere. The best mannered gentlemen would think nothing of lighting up anywhere he chose and if someone didn't come running with an ashtray, he might casually flick the ashes on the floor and drown the butt in a water glass.

Cows huddle up against the cold – just like the smokers!

I can remember walking into a diner, sitting next to one of those petite, beautiful, grandma-looking ladies with that fair, perfect skin, and think nothing about firing up a Lucky, taking a deep drag, and blowing a big stream of smoke through my nose onto her plate of Crepes Suzette. I can also remember seeing those nice old grandmas gasp, fall over on the floor and do the "dead chicken," and think to myself, "I wonder what the heck got into her."

Modern smokers are far more respectful of the nonsmoker. A gentleman will no longer light up without asking permission, and is also keenly aware of non-smoking areas. That is not to say that the rules are not violated now and then. It is common enough to see a high society gal wearing an evening dress too thin for cold weather, duck around a corner in a non-smoking zone, light up a Benson and Hedges, and take a few quick drags. I will have to give these modern gals some credit though, if someone surprises them, they won't just toss the butt on the floor and step on it. Modern women are more apt to spit in their hands, grind the fire out in their palms, and stuff the butt in their bras before walking away with the perfect look of innocence.

It is a good thing spring is only a couple of months away. I don't know who will appreciate it the most, my cows or the smokers!

Up Sims Creek

By: Rod Nelson

Finding a dentist, both personable and cheap, no easy task

Times are tough here at Sims. All I have to do to prove that is to look in the mirror. It requires a good sense of humor just to see that sight every morning. Even though it probably would only cost me 20,000 dollars for a million dollar smile, I just can't afford it.

I don't know if dental care was ever very affordable, but I know it used to be better than it is nowadays.

I needed some dental work when I first moved to Sims. Rather than ask the natives any advise, I just drove to Mandan and looked around for dentist's signs. I drove right past all the dental places that looked like the Taj Mahal. I didn't slow down at any of the dentist's signs in front of shiny, new structures. Finally, right on main street of Mandan I saw a tiny sign that said something like "Dr. Riedinger, DDS."

I parked my car, and walked back to the sign which pointed upstairs. It was a long walk up the creaky stairway and up at the top I met Dr. Riedinger. He was a kindly, older gentleman. It was obvious that he no longer was really trying to get more business, for the most part, he was just taking care of old customers. He no longer had a receptionist, but when I explained my problem he ushered me right back to the chair. The equipment in his office looked like machinery you might find on a solid, dependable, farmer's yard. The kind of farmer who lived within his means, always paid his bills, and had never had a writedown. If I remember right, it was mostly green, had lots of cables and pulleys, and right by the chair was the old-time porcelain sink with running water that you spit into when necessary. One look at his office and I knew I was home!

I liked Doc Riedinger. He did what work I needed, and if I suffered any pain, it was at least, the worst when I was in the chair, not when I paid my bill. I always remember him telling me "Rod, your teeth are wearing nice and evenly, don't let

Finding a dentist, both personable and cheap, no easy task

anyone tell you that you have to spend a lot of money to build them all up."

Darn that old Doc Riedinger, when he was only about 70 he decided he should retire and he did.

I dreaded going to the dentist the next time I needed one. Being somewhat bigoted, I only tried dentists whose names ended in land, vold, vig, or son, thinking that I might find one who still possessed a flicker of conscience and might be affordable. I soon learned that conscience removal courses in modern medical schools are more than effective and none of them are truly affordable.

Chairside manners are lacking alot as well. Actually, I tended to like most of the dentists that I met, but soon tired of them looking into my mouth, doubling over with laughter, and calling everyone in the building over to look in my mouth. "This is what 40 years of Copenhagen will do for you," they would chortle. After they would regain their composure, they would recommend every modern procedure they could think of to properly repair my teeth.

I broke part of a tooth off a couple years ago. Even I realized that I needed a crown. I suppose I could have bought the missus a few less furs and had it fixed, but it galled me to think that I would have to put 63 rides on bronky colts to pay for a couple hours of work.

I interviewed people all over the state about their dentists. "Do you like your dentist?" I would ask. "Oh yes, he does absolutely first class work," they would reply. My next question was always "Does he charge what he is worth?" "Heavens no, his prices are atrocious," was the standard answer.

My tongue was so tired of rasping the jagged edge of my tooth, I finally decided I couldn't stand it any more and made an appointment with an almost local dentist in

Finding a dentist, both personable and cheap, no easy task

Elgin. I liked the fact that there was no receptionist. John and his wife Mary have kind of a "Mom and Pop" dentist shop. John is the dentist and Mary handles everything from the phone to mixing up all the cement that they put in your teeth. I introduced myself, told them my problem and added "I write a column for a paper and will publicly berate you if you charge me too much."

I thanked John for not laughing when he first looked at my teeth. "No mouth is too disgusting for me to look at," he reassured me.

He didn't try to talk me into spending money on anything I didn't think was necessary and went right to work. It wasn't long until he had my mouth filled with pry bars, suction tubes, and a variety of machinery I couldn't explain. Mary chatted pleasantly as she handed John the tools. She likes horses and asked me. "How old should a colt be before they should be trained?" "Glurg," I replied. It wasn't long before I felt like we were old friends and when Mary asked if she could come and sing at the Sims Church some time, I enthusiastically said. "Wug, skuggle ah harg snog."

I just got the permanent cap on a couple of days ago. When I paid my bill they told me to bring my family down for apple pie some time soon. I walked out of the door looking forward to my next cavity.

I really like my new crown although my neighbors are getting tired of me insisting that they take a look at it. Best of all, I only have to ride some bronky colt 33 times to pay for it!.

Up Sims Creek

By: Rod Nelson

Bill can't sew a prom dress, but he sure can patch coveralls

Things look a little better here at Sims. Spring is closer all the time. Looks like my coveralls will make it to warm weather. Of course if you live in the Almont-New Salem area, coveralls last a little longer than many other places.

People like Clara Barton, Florence Nightingale, Jonas Salk and others have become famous for the things they did to improve the health of their fellow man. We have a local fella who has done a lot to protect and improve the health and well being of the local farmers and ranchers of this area.

His name is Bill Duppong. Bill lives in New Salem and his specialty is repairing ripped up chore clothing.

Lets' say you sat in a puddle of battery acid and all of a sudden you notice a draft just where you really hate to have one or perhaps you snagged the zipper on an almost mint condition three-year-old pair of insulated bibs and ruined it. Maybe a mad cow rolled you through a barb wire fence and tore the back out of your Polar King coveralls. Maybe you have worn a favorite garment for so long that it has more holes in it than the box on a 1980 Toyota pickup and you still can't bear to throw it away. No problem, just take it to Bill.

There have been people who have been plagued by runny noses, hacking coughs, and high fevers and have regained complete health just by having Bill patch their chore clothes.

Bill is 86 years old. When he retired from farming twenty some years ago he needed something to do, so he bought a sewing machine and started patching clothes. If you looked at Bill's hands it may be easy to guess that those hands have been wrapped around a lot of pitchforks, shovels, steering wheels, and harness lines. You could easily guess that Bill has done a lot of shocking, cow milking, and the

Bill can't sew a prom dress, but he sure can patch coveralls

multitude of other tasks done on a farm. Even after twenty years of sewing, his hands still don't resemble those of a seamstress.

Perhaps you think it strange that I compare Bill with greats in the medical field but I think it is at least fair to say that Bill is in preventive medicine. He has kept a lot of people a lot warmer and has saved them the pain of buying new chore clothes.

There are other ways that one can compare Bill to doctors. Neither Bill nor the doctors I have known charge what they are worth. The main difference is that Bill charges less.

Bill has repaired a lot of clothing that a Blue Heeler would walk past to lay on a paper feed sack. He has been known to say "Well, it isn't worth it, but I'll try to fix it up."

He always did.

If you needed a new prom dress, suit, or evening gown don't call Bill. In fact don't call Bill for any reason. Bill has plenty to do the way it is without getting new customers. Besides, before he gets too busy, I want to get my coveralls patched so I'm ready for next winter!

Up Sims Creek

By: Rod Nelson

If you're planning on attending bull sales, follow these tips

It is cold, dreary, and miserable here at Sims, but the unmistakable signs of spring are showing up. The signs of spring vary for different people. Long before the weather gets nice and the robins return we are reminded that the season is here.

For lots of people, seed catalogs are telltale signs. For me, bull sale catalogs signal the return of spring. It is a good time of the year to live in the western part of North Dakota. Our cousins in the eastern part of the state who enjoy auctions have to be content to stand humped up in the wind, standing in ankle deep mud to watch a bunch of worn out machinery sell. If they are lucky there is a decent lunch counter where one can purchase a small Styrofoam cup of bad coffee and a day-old doughnut. Out West one can sit in relative comfort in a heated barn, eat a free meal, and view bulls that will never look better than they do on the day of the sale.

Bull sales continue to be good social events, mini-vacations, and culinary delights. There are no shortage of bull sales. I get sale catalogs for breeds of cattle I have never even heard of. It sometimes is hard to decide which bull sales to attend.

A little pre-sale preparation will enhance your bull sale season. Let's say there are two sales on the same day. A simple phone call can give you the information you need. Always ask what they are serving for lunch. Ask how long the lunch counter will be open. It is important to know if one can stand right by the cookies and bars and eat right on through the sale. In some instances, if you call ahead of time you may even make some suggestions about what you would like to have for lunch. Be reasonable, don't ask for Certified Angus Beef at a Bos Indicus sale. If they are serving chicken, don't attend!

Get to know as much about the auctioneers as you can. Avoid those that drone on and on about every bull and insult the crowd if they aren't buying bulls they don't want.

Avoid sales where the owner likes to make speeches about too many bulls. My

If you're planning on attending bull sales, follow these tips

favorite bull sale speaker is Ralph Pederson from Firesteel, SD. Ralph's yearly speech is mainly, "Sure appreciate you folks coming and buy them as cheap as you can."

You can't condemn a fella for talking a little, but beware of those guys who actually believe what they are telling you. Some of them really get carried away especially if they get to talking about the profits you will make by using their bulls. After all, most people who have been in the cattle business a while have heard too many fairy tales about profits.

Get to know the ring men. Don't sit in an area where they take a bid from you every time you reach up to pick your nose.

On the offside chance you are actually interested in purchasing a bull, follow a few rules. Never purchase a bull that you didn't look at prior to the sale. Remember that they always look better in the ring than they do when you get them home.

Probably one of the most important things to consider when purchasing a bull is to get one with a footnote. On many sale catalogs, special mention is made of the bull under the pedigree and EPD information. It may say something like, "The mother to this calf is one of our favorite cows in the herd. This is her tenth bull calf and every one of them have gone in to purebred herds. We have kept all nine of her heifer calves and they are all first rate mothers, good milkers, and extremely docile."

Some sale catalogs have only a few bulls with footnotes and they tend to get expensive. Find a sale catalog that has a footnote on every bull. It is very possible to buy a tail end bull with an excellent footnote. If you bought what you thought was a pretty nice bull last year, but used him pretty hard and wintered him with the cowherd on wheat straw and suddenly realize he looks a lot more like a desert coyote with distemper than the champion you thought he was, it is mighty comforting to dig that old sale catalog out and read "This bull will mature into one of the freest moving, best looking sires in the breed!"

Up Sims Creek

By: Rod Nelson

What's antique to some may be "new" to others

Things are picking up here at Sims. I made another regular trip to Eastern North Dakota and drug another piece of antique equipment to Morton County.

I don't have any set rules on buying equipment. I care little if the equipment on my place rates high in my neighbors eyes. I don't necessarily buy a different piece of machinery when something of mine wears out. Most of my machinery was worn out when I purchased it. I basically purchase a different piece of equipment when whatever I am replacing no longer functions at all.

This time I bought a red tractor. I don't know how much horsepower it has. I didn't know how old it was until after I bought it. I learned it was 37 years old. Still quite a bit younger than me. No doubt, in 1962 I never dreamed I would ever own such a tractor.

I didn't pay much attention to it before I bought it. I did notice the tires held air and the grill was not damaged, so it was a fair bet that it never had been used as a loader tractor.

It was a rare treat to discover that I liked the tractor better after I had purchased it.

This machine has several features that are new to me. It has a muffler with no holes in it and it doesn't sway back and forth when you hit a bump. It has a seat on it like you see only in pictures, no holes in it, and all the padding is still there. It has paint. Pretty darn good paint.

After the crowd at the sale moved on I went back to admire it. I climbed on and tried to figure out how to start it. I was pushing buttons trying to find the glow plugs and darned if I didn't blunder on to a horn! I never had a tractor with a horn before. It actually started when I finally pushed all the right buttons. I learned that it had power steering that worked. I drove around in circles blowing the horn until too many people started to notice. A fella was standing there in stunned silence

What's antique to some may be 'new' to others

when I parked it and shut it off. He only blinked when I explained that I really liked the horn and I thought the missus would be pleased with it as well.

A final inspection revealed that it had four cylinders. Not too many for modern times, but twice as many as the tractor I was replacing. I was really tickled when I learned that it had a cigarette lighter. I don't know if that works, but even the headlights work, so the cigarette lighter probably does as well. I hate to start smoking again but maybe I can find some other use for the lighter

A final boost to my ego came in a short time. A competent looking fella came over and looked the tractor over. I braced myself for the inevitable, "Wow, you paid plenty for this" story, but this guy said "These tractors are rare, a real collector's item. You sure bought it cheap enough!"

I had it home in just a couple of days. No trouble on the road. The highway patrol has seen me coming down I-94 so many times with old machinery on trailers that they don't pay much attention to me anymore. The missus and the kids seemed to like it. All took turns driving it around the yard and blowing the horn.

I haven't had much use for it yet, but with the frost out of the ground here at Sims, I plan to get the post hole digger on it and try it out soon.

The main thing now is to pay for it. I have a 70 John Deere propane and a 720 diesel for sale if anyone is interested. Both run. You can bet they are in excellent condition. Just driven now and then to the Sims Church!

Up Sims Creek

By: Rod Nelson

The only thing dumber than cows are the people who raise them!

Things are picking up here at Sims. The first couple of days of April brought us some nice moisture in the form of a spring snowstorm. There is nothing like a snowstorm to bring lots of thoughts to your mind, especially if you happen to be calving during the snowstorm. If you are calving, you can think around the clock as you aren't apt to be sleeping.

A couple of nights ago as I was riding along trying to check my cattle, I got to thinking about why I like to raise cattle or why I like cows. I almost startled myself when I suddenly realized that I really don't like cows. I like cattle, but I don't like cows.

Cows and I have different ways of thinking. For instance, after I have gone through considerable effort to move my cows to a location as close to "out of the wind" as I can get and do my best to bed them down, my logic tells me the cow would think that this would be a real good place to lay down and have a calf. Some cows do think this way ,but lots of them look the bedding over and say to themselves, "I believe I will trudge a mile through deep snow, find a spot where the wind can't miss me, have my calf in a snow bank, and munch on the afterbirth while Junior freezes to death."

If the weather gets really bad I have to move my cows near a creek. There are some patches of trees on this creek offering pretty fair protection from the wind but the creek has very steep banks along most of it. If a calf tumbles into the creek it rarely can climb out and if I don't happen to find them soon they are goners.

I think that a cow should look the creek over and choose a spot a safe distance from the creek to have her calf, so when he is trying out his new wobbly legs for the first time she won't have to worry about him toppling into the creek.

A cow however, looks the creek over, chooses a spot where the banks are very steep and deep and lays with her tail end hanging over the edge. As she goes into heavy labor she says to herself, "I believe I will just sacrifice this one to the Creek gods!"

The only thing dumber than cows are the people who raise them!

Let's say a couple of cows do calve in the nice spot I have prepared for them. Logic tells me the cow should be thrilled with her new baby and fuss over him and lick him vigorously to dry him off before he gets cold. Most do this, however a certain percentage of cows after giving birth, look back at the steaming, gasping little critter lying under her tail and say to themselves, "That can't be my calf, that calf over there that my friend Bessie is licking must be my calf." By the time I find the two cows claiming the same calf and get the mess straightened out, Junior is about as lively as a Lutheran hymn!

I can understand why a cow with a newborn calf gets mad at a Blue Heeler and wants to chase him away, but when the dog runs behind me to hide, logic tells me that she shouldn't harm me just to get at the dog. Logic tells me that!

I ride along thinking that it was great that EPD's were invented. EPD's are one more way that it is possible to like a cow. "Ya, she's a dumb old bitty but her EPD's are great!" Prior to EPD's the only thing a cow had going for her was her beauty. You had to love a cow for her beauty as it was impossible to love her for her mind.

I ride along muttering to myself that the only thing dumber than a cow are the people who raise them. Then I come around a really well sheltered spot by a patch of chokecherry bushes and spot a cow with a newborn calf. The calf is snuggled up tight against mama on the downwind side. His hair has been licked so much he looks like he has been blow-dried. I shine my flashlight down to the cows bag and can see she has been sucked. The cow gives me a "we are OK but thanks for checking and please stay away" look. Junior looks as contented as the missus at a family reunion.

I ride away into the night smiling to myself and thinking "Gosh, I love that cow!"

Up Sims Creek

By: Rod Nelson

Don't blame cows for shortcomings, blame breeders

Things are picking up here at Sims. Tried out a new thermometer last night. When I checked it this morning it registered seven degrees warmer than my old one. It is somewhat comforting to know that I was warmer than I thought last winter.

I have been troubled a little the last couple of weeks. Ever since I wrote the column on the lack of intelligence in cattle I have had a guilty conscience. I realized it wasn't fair to criticize a poor dumb animal. It is a cheap shot when one picks on someone or something that cannot defend itself. After a couple of days I realized that the cow should not be held responsible for her ignorance. The blame lies squarely on the shoulders of the purebred breeders.

Cattle are domesticated animals. At one time cattle had all the survival instincts of other wild animals. They needed no help to deliver a healthy, vigorous calf and the calf would quickly get to its feet and nurse. A predator had better be on his toes to harm the offspring of those cattle. The mothers would fight to the death to protect their young.

Modern purebred breeders continually strive to destroy the best natural instincts of cattle. Protective mothers are culled for "bad" disposition. Cows that don't know how to lick a new calf to warm him up don't matter to the purebred breeder because someone will be out there to drag the new baby to the warm-up box, give him a good massage, and they will soon heat some colostrum milk to feed the newborn. If the new baby is too stupid to suck, no problem, he gets fed with a stomach tube a couple of times. Most all purebred breeders have a refrigerator filled with frozen colostrum just for those occasions.

If a cow has an udder that is so big and pendulous that a newborn calf can't find a teat, the purebred breeder stands there and pushes the calf's head down until he learns where to find breakfast. The cow gets praise for her "milking ability." The cow stands patiently while this process goes on. She learned to stand patiently the

Don't blame cows for shortcomings, blame breeders

last time she calved and the purebred breeder hand-milked her for two weeks until the calf learned how to suck her balloon teats.

If a modern purebred cow doesn't like what she is fed, no problem, if she doesn't eat, the purebred breeder will find something for her to eat that she likes better.

Instinct used to insure the survival of a species. Modern instinct in cattle is to give birth close to the barn so the purebred breeder doesn't have so far to drag the calf to the warm-up box.

EPDs or Estimated Progeny Differences are numbers assigned to purebred animals to estimate growth, milking ability, birth weights, etc. of their offspring. EPDs are praised as a buyer's tool, but they are probably a better seller's tool. An animal with sterling EPDs however is not always a desirable animal. There are no EPDs for intelligence, disease resistance, or physical handicaps.

Cows from different purebred herds have gotten to know each other at vet clinics. A couple of cows visiting at a vet clinic the other day were overheard saying. "Nice visiting with you, see you again next year when we prolapse."

I can imagine a cow conversation going something like this. "Are you seeing any good looking new bulls this year?" "No," the second cow sniffs, "My children are all from frozen embryos."

I can visualize a cold, raw day and a new mother trying her best to lick her newborn and try to get him on his feet when another cows walks up and tells her. "Really now Daphne, you don't have to do that any more. This is the nineties you know!"

There are still a few good cattle if you look hard enough for them. My friend Bill Larsen from Wyoming told me about a cow he saw while driving on a prairie trail in

Don't blame cows for shortcomings, blame breeders

a remote part of Wyoming. Bill observed a cow shaking her head at him and pawing dirt at least 300 yards from his pickup. "Damn," Bill said in amazement, "That was a good cow."

Bill told me he quit packing scour pills. Bill said, "My cows have horns, sharp horns. I am not going to risk my life just because some stupid calf has a belly ache."

I don't know if this guy is quoted correctly, but I heard my friend Sonny was showing his cattle to someone one day and he said, "This is the most trouble free herd of cattle you will ever see." He then added, "Of course, it took years of neglect to get them that way!"

I have often been envious of buffalo producers. I am sure buffalo possess wonderful survival instincts. I heard a rumor the other day though, that they were developing EPDs for buffalo.

It won't be long until some conscientious buffalo mom will be licking her calf and another buffalo mom will come along and say, "Really now Emma, this is the new millennium, you know!"

Up Sims Creek

By: Rod Nelson

Dad wouldn't have a pickup, he'd just haul everything in the car

Well, its springtime and high school rodeo season here at Sims. My high school freshman is an aspiring calf roper and team roper and my duty is to get him to the rodeos.

A neighbor also has a high school roper and I usually can get him to haul my son's horses. Occasionally, however, the boys get set up on different days and I have to fire up the Dodge, hook up the trailer, and set out on the open highway.

This is easier said than done as the Dodge does not necessarily run when I want it to. Last week I had to have it towed to a mechanic in Glen Ullin to get it ready for a weekend run to Valley City. The mechanic didn't find much wrong with it that wouldn't be consistent with 13 years use and 150,000 miles. He didn't find out what had mysteriously caused it to die out on the Sims hill one day when I was pulling a trailer. It ran fine for him running errands around town. His main comment to the missus when she went to pick it up was "that is the roughest riding pickup I have ever driven, my back still hurts from driving it on smooth pavement!"

Last Saturday morning we made the trek to Valley City. The missus followed us with the car. No problems. We even made it back to Sims before dark. The howling southeastern winds helped a little. I never did decide if I went faster in high gear or when I pushed the clutch in and let the wind push a little.

I was grumbling to myself about the lack of power and general lack of comfort of this vehicle and wondering why I had ever purchased it in the first place when just west of Mandan a couple of carloads of high school prom goers passed me. The glimpse of tuxedos and pretty dresses at first brought waves of nostalgia to me, then it struck me like a thunderbolt that the vehicles I drove were an inherited condition!

Going to the prom back in my day was a tough deal. I don't know which was the hardest. Getting up enough courage to ask some gal to the event, or cleaning up Dad's car!

243

Dad wouldn't have a pickup, he'd just haul everything in the car

We were a one-car family at that time. Dad had a 1 1/2 ton truck and whatever odd brand of car he could find. I was never able to go with Dad when he bought a car, but it never took him long to make a selection. I have always imagined the dialogue Dad and a car salesman might have had.

Dad: "What do you have for used cars?" Salesman: "I have a nice two-year-old Chevrolet with twenty thousand miles on it." Dad: "You wouldn't happen to have any Ramblers or Hudsons would you?" Salesman: "Well we do happen to have a Rambler Ambassador with a V8, power steering, and an automatic transmission." Dad: "Do you have anything with less cylinders and without all that optional junk on it?" Salesman: "I think we have a four-year-old Rambler with a six cylinder, three speed and overdrive." Dad: "I'll take it."

Since Dad didn't think a pickup was worth owning, the family car hauled everything from cream cans, to fencing materials, to salt blocks, or for any type of livestock that would fit through the doors.

Getting those cars ready for a prom was a major problem.

The first major task was to unload the car. Wire stretchers, fencing pliers, bolts, milk strainers, oil cans, harness parts, empty vaccine bottles, assorted junk. All had to be removed and taken to the proper buildings. Car cleaning usually solved some mysteries like: "Hey Dad, Remember that can of KRS you couldn't find? Found it under the seat. Not too much leaked out of it either." Or, "Say Mom, do you remember that bundle of bananas you couldn't find a couple of weeks ago?"

The next step was the once-a-year washing. This was no easy task The car may be coated with a variety of grime. It may cause a comment like, "Hey Dad, don't park this thing under the highline wire again 'til after the prom will you," or "Hey Dad, what are you feeding those cows anyway!"

Dad wouldn't have a pickup, he'd just haul everything in the car

After borrowing Mom's vacuum cleaner and sucking out all the inside dust, the windows and dash were carefully washed. Mom, no doubt thinking of my date's welfare, always loaned me a decent blanket to cover the front seat.

I suppose the old cars were presentable enough by the time I picked up my date, but I never remember being very proud of them. If my dates ever leaned over and melted into my shoulder I always knew they didn't have much of a tolerance for carbon monoxide, or if they jumped when I tried to give them a kiss I was never sure if it was from excitement or if they happened to sit on a staple that I hadn't found!

As my Dodge ground down I-94 last weekend, I gazed down at the cluttered floorboards and thought to myself. "The folks never had to worry about me going 'steady' when I was too young. One date with me was enough!"

Up Sims Creek

By: Rod Nelson

At age 25, 50 seemed old – now 50 is just middle age

As I write this, I am halfway through my 50th birthday. Just to see Sims this wet is quite a birthday treat! So far I have received four presents. One can only imagine how many I may receive by midnight.

Two of my presents are books. One is a biography of Will Rogers and the other is about some old duffer named Bill Bryson who wrote a book about walking the Appalachian Trail. I read several chapters out of each of them today.

Both books are interesting and somewhat inspired me. No, I am not interested in walking the Appalachian Trail, but I just may ride to Oklahoma some day.

I have often wondered how I could reach the age of fifty and not have experienced all the things I have wanted to do. Just existing in North Dakota has been a full time job for me.

I can't remember all of the last fifty years. I have enough trouble remembering the last twenty-five. I do remember part of my wish list when I was only half this old. I know I hoped to become a great bronc rider some day and I hoped to have the opportunity to spend at least one winter in a cold climate, some place like the Yukon where I would slide through the forest behind a team of Huskies and experience the thrills of breathing air that was 70 degrees below zero.

I suppose the only thing that kept me from being a great bronc rider has been an acute lack of talent. I don't know what kept me from the Yukon, perhaps I have been softened too much from 15 years of living in balmy Southern North Dakota.

I am perhaps more surprised with the things that did happen to me, changes in my life I did not expect.

When I was twenty-five years old, I never expected to have any hair on my chest, or at least never expected it to move there from the top of my head!

At age 25, 50 seemed old – now 50 is just middle age

When I was twenty-five years old, I some times fantasized that maybe some day I would reach 200 pounds. Twenty five years later one of my greatest wishes is to weigh 200 pounds again!

When I was twenty-five years old, I never imagined that the warm glow in my cheeks would move to my knees.

When I was twenty-five years old, I never expected to be known as a poet.

When I was twenty five years old I thought 50-year-olds were old duffers. At age 50 I am hoping 50 is merely middle age. If it isn't, I am acutely aware I am already too old to have a mid-life crisis.

When I was wenty-five years old, I never thought much about retirement. I still don't think much about it. I only hope to enjoy good enough health to work if I live that long.

I am still not old enough to worry too much about the future. I want to enjoy a few things first.

I sure hope I can have a little fun this summer. I plan to go to a few good brandings. I hope I can get to a few ropings. I want to lose enough weight so I can go to that foot race in Bismarck and hopefully beat that fat guy who humiliated me last year.

For the future: Well, I'd sure like to be a great bronc rider someday, and someday I sure hope I can spend a winter in a cold climate!